whalewatcher

Trevor Day

Published by the Natural History Museum, London

To Bronya, Anouska and Indiarose in the hope that when they are old enough to
watch the wonderful mammals described in this book, the animals are still there
to be seen.

First published in the UK in 2006 by
The Natural History Museum
Cromwell Road
London SW7 5BD
www.nhm.ac.uk

A Marshall Edition
Conceived, edited and designed by Marshall Editions
The Old Brewery
6 Blundell Street
London N7 9BH
UK
www.quarto.com

ISBN: 0 565 09212 X
ISBN 13: 978 0 565 09212 2
A catalogue record for this book is available from the British Library.

Originated in Hong Kong by Modern Age
Printed and bound in China

Publisher: Richard Green
Commissioning Editor: Claudia Martin
Art Direction: Ivo Marloh
Editor: Johanna Geary
Picture Manager: Veneta Bullen
Design: Alchemedia
Indexer: Hilary Bird
Production: Nikki Ingram

Contents

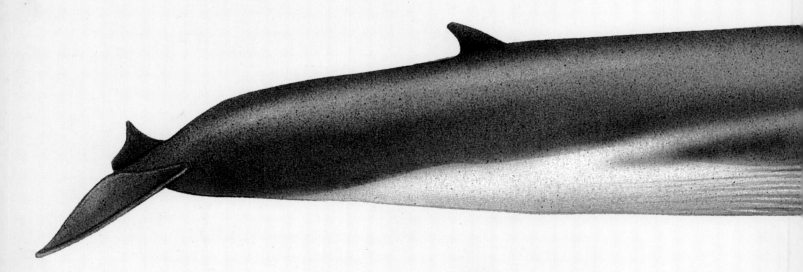

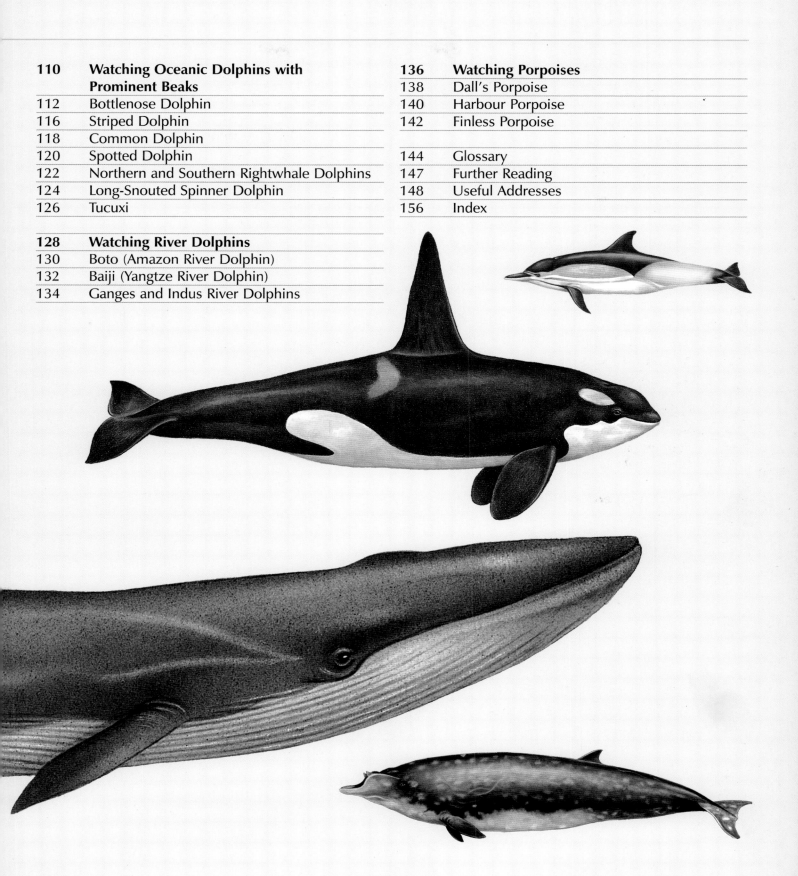

An Introduction to Watching

In the last 50 years, people's attitudes to whales have undergone a sea change. Thankfully, many people across the world would now rather watch whales, and appreciate their beauty, bulk and extraordinary behaviour, than hunt them.

Whales (and their smaller relatives, the dolphins and porpoises) also inspire in us feelings of kinship. When you hear the breath of a whale at close range, you are forcefully reminded that they are air-breathing mammals, like us. When you watch a school of bottlenose dolphins duck and weave, you realise they are complex animals with sophisticated behaviour. The strength and complexity of their friendships and family ties may also be likened to our own. And many whales and dolphins have a strange curiosity about people, which is all the more surprising given our long history of ruthlessly exploiting them.

Whale watching, as a pastime and a tourist industry, began to emerge in the mid-1950s, when Californians took a keen interest in the grey whales that migrated along their coastline. Today, more than 10 million people a year join commercial whale-watching trips in one or more of up to 90 nations. The range of opportunities to watch whales, dolphins or porpoises is astonishingly wide, and includes watching from the shore, from a floating vessel, from the air or, on rare occasions, while actually in the water.

The aim of this book is to provide an introduction to the broad range of whale-watching opportunities around the world and to offer a starting point for planning your whale-watching trip of a lifetime. All the world's whales, dolphins and porpoises are listed here, with information on where and how to see the more common, recognisable and accessible species.

Left: The broad tail, or flukes, of a humpback whale in Frederick Sound, Alaska, where humpbacks are watchable on their feeding grounds in summer months.

What Is a Cetacean?

Whales, dolphins and porpoises are collectively known as cetaceans, after the scientific group of marine mammals, the order Cetacea, to which they belong. The other two marine mammal orders are the sea cows, or sirenians (Sirenia), which includes manatees and the dugong, and the pinnipeds (Pinnipedia), which includes seals, sea lions and the walrus. As mammals, all marine mammals, like ourselves, are warm-blooded, breathe air using lungs, have some hair and suckle their young with milk. Scientifically, all cetaceans are whales but, by general agreement, people call some scientific families of smaller whales dolphins, and one family of small whales porpoises.

ORIGINS

Modern cetaceans are descended from land-living hoofed mammals called even-toed ungulates. Today, this group includes cows, camels and hippopotamuses, with hippopotamuses as the closest living relatives of cetaceans.

The evolution of land-living hoofed mammals into modern whales began at least 60 million years ago. By 55 million years ago, ancient whales, called archaeocetes, were evolving from hairy amphibious four-legged ancestors that probably looked like giant otters. Over the next 20 million years, their forelimbs gradually became flippers, tails broadened into horizontal flukes, nostrils moved to the top of the head to form a blowhole and hind limbs and hair all but disappeared. These changes enabled early cetaceans to cut their ties with the land and master swimming and breathing in water.

WHAT IS A WHALE?

Like large fish, such as sharks, cetaceans are adapted for swimming through water. They have streamlined bodies to reduce drag; fins for steering, braking and adjusting trim; and a propulsive tail to drive themselves forward. But although they are superficially alike, fish and whales are in fact very different. Fish are cold-blooded, they extract oxygen from water using gills and they swim by moving a vertically flattened tail from side to side. Whales, by contrast, are warm-blooded and breathe oxygen from the air through nostrils. Their nostrils emerge through one or two blowholes at the top of their heads. Whales have horizontally flattened tails, which they move up and down to swim.

Below: A Bryde's whale, a baleen whale, showing some of the major physical characteristics of cetaceans.

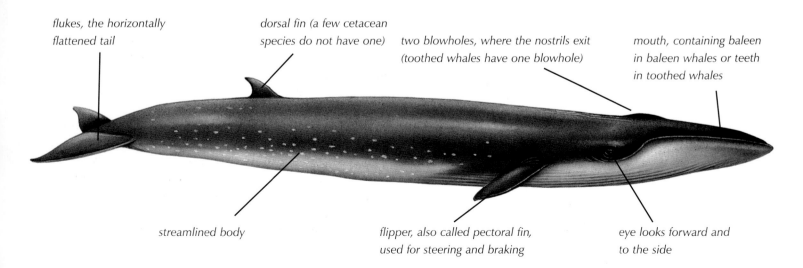

flukes, the horizontally flattened tail

dorsal fin (a few cetacean species do not have one)

two blowholes, where the nostrils exit (toothed whales have one blowhole)

mouth, containing baleen in baleen whales or teeth in toothed whales

streamlined body

flipper, also called pectoral fin, used for steering and braking

eye looks forward and to the side

BALEEN OR TOOTHED WHALE?

The 85 or so species of modern cetaceans fall into two scientific groups. About 15 species are baleen whales (members of the suborder Mysticeti) that capture their food using baleen – hundreds of baleen plates, or whalebone, that hang from the upper jaw. The plates are made of keratin, the same protein ingredient found in hair, nails and horn. The baleen plates are frayed on the inner edges to form a forest of bristles that strain small animals – typically fish or animal plankton – from seawater. When feeding, baleen whales squeeze engulfed water through the baleen, trapping prey on the bristles. The very biggest whales – including blue, fin and bowhead whales – capture some of the smallest animals in the sea.

About 71 species of cetaceans, including the dolphins and porpoises, are toothed whales (suborder Odontoceti). The number of teeth varies greatly between species. The narwhal, for example, has no functional teeth, but adult males have one tooth (occasionally two) that grows forward as a tusk. Spinner dolphins, on the other hand, have more than 170 teeth. Toothed whales use their teeth to bite and grasp prey, but they swallow their food whole or in large chunks.

Toothed whales differ from baleen whales in other ways: toothed whales have one blowhole while baleen whales have two.

Above: A grey whale with its mouth open. Its baleen, used for filtering small animals from the water, is clearly visible hanging from the upper jaw.

Above: The teeth of a killer whale. Toothed whales use their teeth for grasping and biting rather than chewing.

DOLPHIN OR PORPOISE?

Dolphins and porpoises are small toothed whales. Members of five of the toothed whale families are called 'dolphins'. Dolphins, if you can look inside their mouths, have cone-shaped teeth and most, but not all, have a prominent beak. The four species of river dolphins are spread among four families (Pontoporiidae, Platanistidae, Lipotidae and Iniidae), while the 32 or so species of oceanic dolphin all belong to the true dolphin family, the Delphinidae. By contrast, the six species of porpoise (family Phocoenidae) have blunt heads and their teeth are fat with rounded sides, bulging rather like the blade of an old-fashioned digging spade (and like the symbol for the spade suit of cards).

To add confusion, not all members of the true dolphin family (Delphinidae) are called dolphins. Six large species that have bulbous foreheads were called 'blackfish' by early whalers, because of their dark coloration. Four of the six blackfish species reach the size of whales, weighing at least a tonne, but the two smallest species, the pygmy killer whale and the melon-headed whale, remain the size of dolphins. By convention, all blackfish are called whales.

ANATOMY

The anatomy of cetaceans is different from that of the land-living mammals from which they evolved, because the properties of water are so different from those of air. As water, for example, is extremely dense and therefore much more strenuous to move through than air, cetaceans are streamlined to reduce drag.

Examine a cetacean skeleton and it is clear that, in comparison to a four-legged land-living mammal, the hind limbs are missing. The tail is large for propulsion, and the skull and jawbones are elongated. Close examination of the skull reveals that the nasal passages open at the top of the head, enabling the animal to breathe with only the top of its head above water. The forelimbs of cetaceans contain the same arrangement of bones as is found in the forearms or forelegs of land mammals, but the 'arm' and 'hand' bones are shortened while the 'finger' bones are elongated to support a paddle-shaped flipper.

Water conducts heat much more readily than air. Instead of fur, cetaceans have a thick, fat-rich layer of tissue between their internal organs and their skin to trap heat inside the body. This tissue, called blubber, is also a great reserve of chemical energy that the cetacean can 'burn' to power movement and keep itself warm.

SENSES

Sound travels farther and faster in water than in air, while the reverse holds true for light. Light is sparse at depths beyond a few hundred feet and is rapidly filtered by murky water. At night, of course, little or no light penetrates. Hearing is the cetacean's dominant sense underwater. By relying on hearing, and to a lesser extent on touch, whales can find their way about in darkness.

Right: An Atlantic spotted dolphin using echolocation to scan beneath the sand for buried fish.

Toothed whales employ a remarkable remote-sensing mechanism, called echolocation, to navigate. They project pulses of sound through the forehead and listen for the returning echoes, which in many species are channelled through the lower jaw. The time taken for echoes to return gives a measure of distance to nearby reflective objects. The quality of the echoes allows the animal to judge the shape, size, texture and movement of nearby objects. In this way, toothed whales can 'see' their prey using sound and can build up a 'sound picture' of their surroundings. This natural sonar is far more sophisticated than any that military experts have devised. Baleen whales may also be able to echolocate, but this has yet to be convincingly demonstrated.

Eyesight is important to most whales, and their eye components can change shape to focus in air or water. Taste may be important in sampling food, but the sense of smell is probably poor. Cetaceans have a strong geomagnetic sense. They can navigate by invisible lines of magnetic force in the seascape.

DIVING

Cetaceans have a wide range of adaptations to help them stay underwater for long periods before returning to the surface to breathe. Blood and muscle that are rich in oxygen-binding chemicals slowly release oxygen while the whale is underwater. When submerged, some of the whale's blood vessels narrow while others open wide, diverting blood away from the skin, where valuable heat would be lost, and into the core of the animal, especially to the heart and brain to keep them warm and well supplied with oxygen.

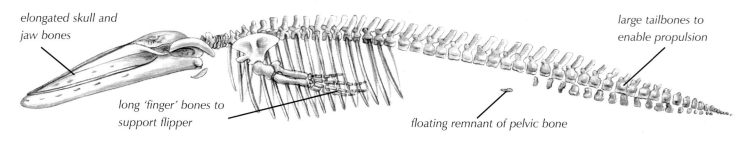

elongated skull and jaw bones

long 'finger' bones to support flipper

floating remnant of pelvic bone

large tailbones to enable propulsion

Above: The skeleton of a blue whale. The elongated skull and jawbones support baleen (not shown) and create a streamlined head shape that cuts through the water with ease. The middle and tail sections of the backbone have large extensions for the attachment of powerful locomotory muscles. The hind limbs and supporting pelvis are absent, although remnants exist in the form of tiny bones that float unattached.

Life Cycle

The smallest cetaceans, such as harbour porpoises, commonly live for about 10 years, but the largest, such as bowhead whales, may live to be well over 100. Almost all cetaceans are social, and the lives of individuals cannot be readily understood without reference to their relationships with others. The more cetaceans are studied in detail, the more complex become the differences in social lives between species, and even between different populations of the same species. Such diversity and the difficulty of interpreting the behaviour of complex social animals are among the major challenges and attractions of whale watching.

BIRTH AND SUCKLING

Gestation, the period of time between conception and birth of offspring, is lengthy in cetaceans. It ranges between about eight and 11 months in small cetaceans, such as the harbour porpoise, and up to 16 months in some larger species, such as the killer whale. The long gestation period reflects the necessity for a newborn whale calf to be well developed and able to swim with its mother from birth.

A cetacean mother typically gives birth to only one calf at a time, and she may not bear a calf again for several years if food supplies are variable, or if she is taking on other roles within the family group. Calves are usually born tail first, which may be an adaptation to enable the calf to rely on oxygenated blood from the mother's placenta until the last moment. Once its head is clear, the calf swims to the surface to take its first gulp of air, often guided from below by its mother.

Most cetacean mothers nurse their calves for six to 12 months, a period during which a calf gains protection from its mother and also learns how to graze plankton or hunt prey and interact with other members of its species. In many species of cetacean, the first year of life is the one most fraught with danger, with some calves succumbing to attacks by sharks or predatory whales such as killer whales.

Below: A humpback whale with her young calf. The calf is less than 5 m (16 ft) long and weighs 1–2 tonnes. The mother probably weighs 20–30 tonnes.

Cetacean milk is fat-rich, and by feeding little and often, the calf grows rapidly and can develop a thick layer of blubber within weeks. Young blue whales can gain an astonishing 90 kg (200 lbs) of body mass each day during their first few months, relying largely on their mother's milk.

FAMILY AND SOCIAL LIFE

Most cetaceans are social animals and form groups, with mother-and-calf pairs as the basic family unit. Some toothed whale species occasionally gather in giant schools of hundreds or thousands of individuals, stretching for many miles across the vast expanse of the ocean.

The social behaviour of cetaceans is shaped by three priorities: to feed, to mate and reproduce, and to avoid predators. It is hazardous to generalise about cetacean social groups because they vary from one species to another, and even within different populations of the same species, as in the case of killer whales and bottlenose dolphins.

Most baleen whales, because of their large size, have few predators except for killer whales and (still occasionally) humans. Their social organisation is shaped largely by the imperatives of finding enough food and, as adults, mating and rearing young. Slow-moving coastal whales, such as the humpback and southern right whales, are among those that have been most extensively studied because they are more easily tracked and observed. Even comparing these two species, there are marked differences. On breeding grounds, male humpbacks compete violently with each other to gain access to a receptive female and become her escort. Aggressive actions include blowing bubbles at each other or swiping one another with a barnacled chin that is used in the manner of a club. Male southern right whales, on the other hand, seem to cooperate rather than physically compete. They herd a female into a restricted area near the coast where one male after another mates with her. Inside the female, however, the sperm from different males vie with each other to be the one that fertilises the female's egg cell.

Above: Atlantic spotted dolphins mating belly to belly. The younger male is beneath the older female.

Among toothed whale species, the size of groups may be a balance between the need to locate enough food and the challenge of avoiding predators. Too many individuals in a group and there may not be enough food to go around when a school of fish or squid is located. Too few, and the group may be vulnerable to attacks from sharks or killer whales. Coastal bottlenose dolphins, for example, form groups of up to 20 individuals, which is a big enough school to fend off most predators, but is not too big to prevent all from sharing in the spoils of finding a small school of fish.

Undoubtedly there are friendships between individuals of the same cetacean species that may or may not be based on family ties. Among southern right whales, for example, mothers with calves seem to gather in friendship groups, warding off individuals that are deemed unacceptable. Among bottlenose dolphins, adult males form friendship groups that can last throughout their adult lives. There are numerous instances among toothed whale species of individuals staunchly caring for or defending a sick or injured group member. In evolutionary terms, this is understandable if the threatened companion is closely related to its carer or defender and they both share many of the same genes. This close genetic relationship, however, does not always apply.

MATING

Among toothed whales, females usually form the stable centre of a group. Immature males grow up within the group before leaving to join other groups, so preventing inbreeding. Killer whales and pilot whales are exceptions to this rule, as closely knit family groups (pods) stay together and males breed with females of other groups when two or more pods temporarily merge.

Strong social ties within groups can result in complex cooperative hunting behaviour, as found in killer whales and some bottlenose dolphins and common dolphins. Such strong social ties also give rise to mass strandings, common among pilot whales and false killer whales, when an entire group stays with a stranded member and all run aground.

Despite all this cooperation and good nature, when it comes to mating there may be intense rivalry between males. Many male toothed whales, especially beaked whales, bear the scars of tooth rakes inflicted by rival males. In many toothed whale societies there are hierarchies, with dominant males having access to most or all of the available females.

On breeding grounds, dominant males almost invariably mate with more than one female. In a given season, a female may have only one mating partner (for example, in narwhals, sperm whales and killer whales) or several (as in right and grey whales and most oceanic dolphin species).

Species mate belly to belly, and large cetaceans, such as baleen whales, mate by swimming side by side and tilting toward one another. Although courtship can last hours or days, the mating act itself is usually brief, lasting a few seconds, but may be repeated several times by the same pair.

Below: Hundreds of belugas gathering in an estuary. Within large aggregations, females and their calves usually stay in groups separate from adult males.

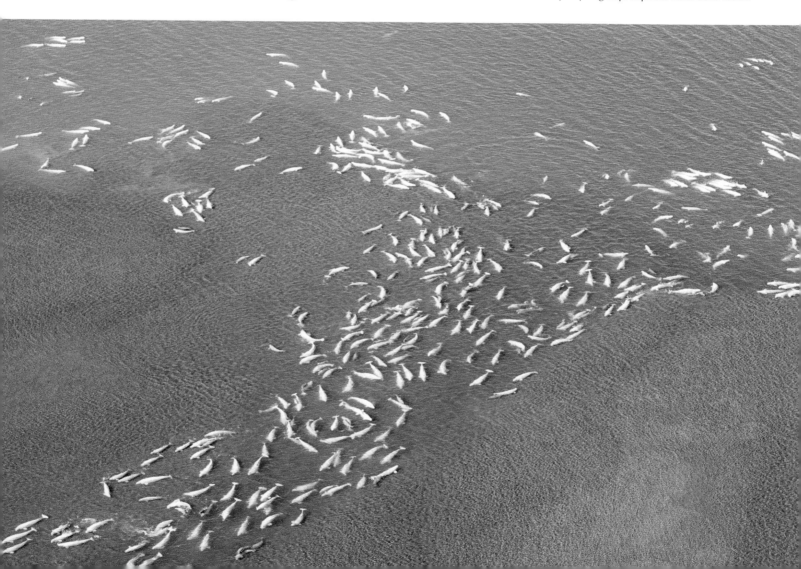

MIGRATION ROUTES OF HUMPBACK WHALES

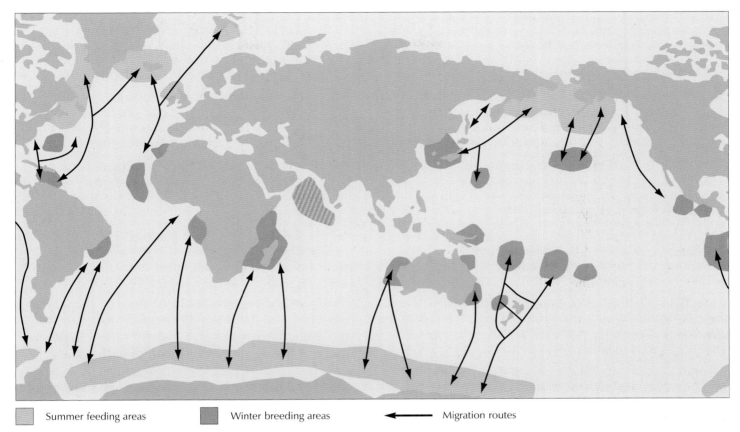

| | Summer feeding areas | | Winter breeding areas | ← | Migration routes |

Above: Populations of humpback whales migrate between cool summer feeding grounds and warm winter breeding grounds in the two hemispheres.

MIGRATION

Where it occurs, migration, or the regular large-scale movement of animals from one location to another, is generally driven by the pursuit of food on the one hand, and the need for safe mating and calving grounds on the other.

Baleen whales, with the possible exception of Bryde's whales and some populations of blue, fin and humpback whales, undergo long-distance migrations from summer feeding grounds in cooler waters to winter breeding grounds in warmer waters. The marathon migrators are humpback whales and grey whales, with some making round trips of more than 18,000 km (11,000 miles) over the course of a year. Migrating in this manner ensures that the whales reach feeding grounds when blooms of plant plankton are at their greatest. This abundance of microscopic plant life fuels an explosion in the growth of animal plankton, which are the favoured food of most baleen whales. Schooling fish, such as herring, also gather to feed on the rich plankton, and they too provide food for baleen whales.

Possible reasons why baleen whales favour warm water for mating and calving are that killer whales, a potential threat to their young, generally prefer cooler waters, and that newborn whales have thin blubber. Calves can develop their thick insulating layer of blubber as they migrate from warm to cool waters, all the while suckling their mother's milk. Of course, some whales spend their entire lives in cool waters and their calves are able to cope. It may be that the long-distance migrations are a legacy from a time when the start and end points of migration runs were much closer, before they became more widely separated by continental drift.

Most toothed whales do not make such regular long-distance migrations, instead making shorter seasonal journeys to intercept prey congregations. Large male sperm whales are a conspicuous exception, leaving warmer waters in summer and migrating to high-latitude seas to feed on squid, before returning to join females and immature males in lower-latitude waters in the winter.

Communication

Social bonds between the individuals in a group are developed and maintained by communication through sight, sound and touch. In cetaceans, as in humans, gestures, postures, direct contact and a wide repertoire of sounds all have meaning. Interpreting the meaning is tricky. Among bottlenose dolphins, for example, what could be taken for aggressive behaviour in one context – biting, ramming, slapping with a tail, making squawking sounds and forcefully blowing bubbles through the blowhole – could be playful behaviour in another. When attempting to interpret behaviour, the context of an encounter – the overriding activity or setting – and the roles of the individuals involved must be considered.

BODY LANGUAGE

Cetaceans may not have vocal language, in the sense of using a structured order of sounds with grammar to convey specific meanings, but that is not to say that their communication is not highly complex. Much of the dance of communication that goes on between individuals of the same cetacean species still remains a mystery to us. Among the more obvious gestures is how one individual orients its body toward another.

In southern right whales, for example, if one whale turns its back on another and points its flukes, it is a warning not to approach. Among bottlenose dolphins, if individuals approach each other head on or at right angles, then the encounter is likely to be an aggressive one. If the two approach at a shallow angle, coming alongside one another, the interaction is more likely to be playful.

TOUCH

Physical contact between individuals of the same species is important in forming and strengthening social bonds. A mother and young calf are commonly in almost constant touch, with contact gradually or abruptly decreasing as the calf becomes weaned and more independent. In bottlenose dolphins, two individuals rubbing bodies together is a sign of affection, and an older dolphin may rub itself against a younger individual to calm it down when agitated. When two dolphins greet each other in a friendly manner, they rub flipper to flipper. Using a flipper to gently touch another dolphin on the flank, between dorsal fin and flukes, is usually a request for help in some endeavour.

SOUND

Cetaceans produce sounds in the air passages and nasal sacs beneath the blowhole and, in toothed whales, these are projected through an oil-filled sac, the melon, at the front of the head. Sounds vary from high-frequency whistles and squeaks to low-frequency rumbles, bellows, grunts and snorts. Toothed whales also use streams of clicks for echolocation. In addition, cetaceans make sounds in other ways: dolphins by jaw-clapping, and most cetaceans by splashing or slapping on the water surface.

In bottlenose dolphins, each individual has its own 'signature' whistle that others in the social group recognise. Chirps, resembling the sounds made by songbirds, probably convey the individual's state of excitement. Squawks, on the other hand, reveal irritation or anger.

While in their breeding grounds, male humpback whales sing complex songs that can last up to 30 minutes or so and follow an overall theme that is shared by others in the same population, but with subtle differences. The songs evolve as the season progresses, and they probably serve to attract females and warn off rival males. As in other baleen whales, the lower-frequency sounds made by humpback whales – some of which are beyond the range of human hearing – may travel hundreds, perhaps thousands, of miles across the ocean. As always, the exact meaning of a communication depends on context: the setting, roles and relationships of the individuals involved.

Right: Oceanic dolphins engaging in head-to-head contact and crossing at right angles, suggesting a combative rather than playful encounter.

Behaviour

What do whales or dolphins do all day? In most cases, they search for food, care for their young, avoid predators and perhaps play and socialise with other members of their group. Our knowledge of whale behaviour is based largely on what we see them do at or near the water surface. But this is just a fraction of their behaviour. Scientists can attach radio tags and cameras to cetaceans to track their underwater movements and use underwater microphones – hydrophones – to record the chorus of sounds cetaceans make. Nevertheless, on a whale-watching trip, there is plenty of behaviour for you to see, hear and interpret.

BREACHING AND PORPOISING

Many whales and dolphins, at one time or another, fling themselves out of the water and crash back in, an act known as 'breaching'. When a large whale belly-flops into the water, the resounding splash and slap can be seen and heard for hundreds of yards. Some dolphins leap high and do somersaults, and when one animal in a group breaches, others may follow suit. Whale experts have recorded humpback whales and dolphins breaching more than 100 times in a single display.

Breaching probably serves different purposes on different occasions. Sometimes it may be a warning to other individuals or a defence against predators. Some whales and dolphins breach to herd prey into a tight school to make them easier to catch. Some animals breach to dislodge skin parasites, or perhaps simply for fun.

Above: A southern right whale about to slap its flipper. Depending on the severity of the slap, this could be leisurely, playful or aggressive behaviour.

Smaller cetaceans leap out of the water in a graceful arc. Spinner dolphins not only leap, but spin at the same time. Leaping can have a general meaning, perhaps indicating a state of excitement, or specific significance. Off Argentina, dusky dolphins leap to indicate a local school of fish and to signal other dolphins to converge and help herd the fish before feeding begins.

'Porpoising' is repeated leaping as a cetacean travels from one place to another. It is carried out not just by porpoises, but also by dolphins and even small whales

Above: Killer whale breaching near the San Juan Islands, Washington State. This could be a leap for joy or an aggressive gesture, or serve some other purpose.

such as killer and pilot whales. With each leap, the animal breathes, and because air offers less resistance to movement than water, graceful porpoising can be a highly efficient method of travel.

FLIPPER-SLAPPING

'Flipper-slapping' – slapping flippers against the sea surface – can create plenty of noise and spray and, like breaching, may have different meanings at different times. In humpback whales, leisurely flipper-slapping is often used as part of courtship, while more violent slapping may be a deterrent to rival males.

FLUKING AND LOBTAILING

Cetaceans sometimes lift their flukes above the water surface as they angle their head downward to launch a deep dive. This behaviour is called 'fluking'. Whether the flukes are raised high ('flukes up') or bent over ('flukes down') tends to be characteristic for a given species. The type of fluking, and the shape of the tail flukes that this activity reveals, are both very helpful identification features.

Above: A humpback whale dramatically lobtailing in Frederick Sound, Alaska.

Below: A bottlenose dolphin 'playing' with an octopus in the Red Sea. Such play may sharpen reflexes and coordination in preparation for hunting.

Many cetaceans also lift their flukes out of the water and slap them down on the water surface, called 'lobtailing'. This may be repeated many times in a row. Similar to lobtailing is 'tail-breaching', when the tail flops down rather than being slapped down. Both lobtailing and tail-breaching can be aggressive actions. A male humpback whale may lobtail or tail-breach at rival males, and whales sometimes lobtail when boats come too close. Sometimes, however, lobtailing is done slowly, carefully and playfully.

PLAYING

When we see dolphins exuberantly darting and twisting through the water, leaping through the air and chasing one another, it is difficult not to imagine that they are 'playing'. However, even what appears to be play for its own sake may serve important functions.

Through play, animals learn how to socialise with other members of their group, they develop family and friendship bonds, they improve coordination and they practise hunting. They may even develop tools. In the 1990s, bottlenose dolphins were observed using a sponge to protect the tip of the snout as they probed for animals buried in the sandy seabed of Shark Bay, Western Australia.

LOGGING

Some species of whale, including pilot whales, sperm whales and various beaked whales, are well-known for 'logging'. When engaged in this behaviour, a group of whales floats motionless at the surface, with all individuals facing the same direction. It is quite likely they are sleeping, or rather 'cat-napping', which is what cetaceans do in place of proper sleep.

Above: A pod of Baird's beaked whales logging off the coast of Isla Guadalupe, Mexico.

Above: A beluga spyhopping. The animal may be curious, anxious or simply trying to get its bearings.

Above: Atlantic spotted dolphins bow-riding in the Bahamas. Bow-riding offers an opportunity for individuals to confirm their position in the hierarchy.

SPYHOPPING

Many species of cetacean, especially those that frequent coastal waters, 'spyhop'. They raise their heads slowly out of the water and look around. Spyhopping probably enables them to orient themselves or find the source of a disturbance. Killer whales spyhop when they intend to hunt animals that are hauled up on shore or on ice floes. Whales sometimes spyhop when they are disturbed by vessels.

WAKE- AND BOW-RIDING

'Bow-riding', riding seemingly effortlessly on the pressure wave in front of a moving vessel, is a popular pastime for many dolphins. Such behaviour offers opportunities to reinforce the social bonds and pecking order in the group. Males may jostle other males out of the way and frolic with receptive females. 'Wake-riding', swimming in a vessel's V-shaped wake, provides an opportunity for dolphins to play.

Above: More than a dozen humpback whales bubble-net feeding for herring in Frederick Sound, Alaska.

FEEDING

Knowledge about what a cetacean feeds on, and how it feeds, is invaluable when identifying animals at sea. Baleen whales feed on small planktonic (drifting) animals, on schooling fish or, in the exceptional case of the grey whale, on bottom-living animals. Rorqual whales gulp-feed, bowhead and right whales skim-feed and sei whales do both. Find high concentrations of the whale's food and there is a fair chance of finding the whale. Schools of herring, sardines and other bait fish attract not just baleen whales, but diving birds, seals, sharks, tuna and toothed whales as well. Look for birds wheeling and diving, and a concentration of bait fish may well lie just beneath the sea surface.

When watching toothed whales, whether killer whales attacking other cetaceans or dolphins herding fish, knowing which feeding strategies are associated with which cetacean is one means of identifying species.

Responsible Watching

Other than watching from the shore or from fixed platforms such as piers, seagoing vessels provide the best opportunities for viewing whales. On balance, scientists and conservationists see well-managed whale watching as a benefit to the well-being of cetaceans. Whale watching is a marvellous way for you to find out about the lives of cetaceans and to gain a greater understanding of the conservation issues facing these animals and the ocean realm at large. Wherever and whenever you go whale watching, and whoever you go with, the golden rule is 'other than your own safety, the welfare of the animals you are watching should always come first'. Be patient and disturb the animals as little as possible.

RESPECT

Threats to cetaceans from badly organised whale-watching trips are mainly a result of poor boat handling, which restricts the free movement of animals while they are being viewed. The prime time to see many cetaceans is when they are on breeding grounds, where they go to mate or give birth. At such times the whales are particularly sensitive to disturbance. Intrusive whale watching can create stress between mother and calf, and even separate them. Noise from vessels can disrupt normal hunting and diving behaviour. In the worst cases, inappropriate whale watching can kill or injure whales, through collision or raking from propeller blades, or lead whales to abandon a locality, threatening the lives of their present and future offspring.

Below: A whale-watching vessel should approach a whale slowly, from behind and to one side, and not get too close.

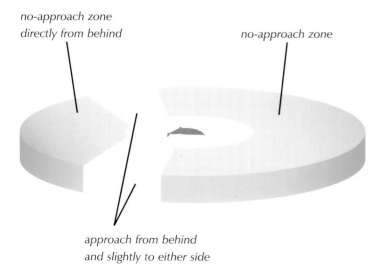

no-approach zone
directly from behind

no-approach zone

approach from behind
and slightly to either side

THE RIGHT EQUIPMENT

Take a range of protective clothing options (several layers) to cover all weather possibilities. You will need equipment to make observations and record your findings. Safety is important. It is better to be over- than underprepared. The minimum equipment for joining a boat trip is:

1. Hat (for warmth and/or sun protection)
2. Waterproof jacket and trousers, rubber-soled deck shoes
3. Life jacket
4. Binoculars (up to 10x magnification)
5. A reliable whale-watching guidebook
6. A recording notebook, pencil and pencil sharpener
7. Sunglasses with polarising lenses
8. Wristwatch and compass
9. Camera with zoom lens and fast-action capability
10. Sunscreen and seasickness tablets
11. Food and drink
12. A waterproof bag to carry all you need

Ultimately, it is in the best interests of whale-watching operators to behave responsibly to ensure that the resource they are encouraging people to see – the whales themselves – remains in, or returns to, the vicinity. So, what is good practice? Different guidelines and regulations operate in different parts of the world, but good practice includes the following:
• **Always let the animals determine their own path and behaviour.** A vessel should approach whales from behind and slightly to one side, not directly from the front or back. The vessel should be manuoeuvred to no closer than 100 m (330 ft). As the vessel gets closer it

should proceed at slow speed on a parallel course with the whale. Vessels should not chase the animals or try to separate the individuals in a group, nor should they crowd the animals into a confined space or surround them. Any boat movement close to whales needs to be slow and deliberate, without sudden changes in direction. Let whales, dolphins and porpoises approach if they want to and then shut off the boat's engines or go into neutral. Limit the time of the interaction and leave the area at 'no wake' speed.

• **Whale watching is an 'eyes on, hands off' activity.** Do not touch or feed whales, dolphins or porpoises.

• **Stay quiet.** Noise may disturb cetaceans, causing stress and altering their natural behaviour. Sound travels well through water and cetaceans are sensitive to it. That said, operators do take care to ensure that whales are aware of your presence. They do not wish to surprise whales or cause an unaware whale to come crashing down on the boat by accident as it breaches.

• **Be litter aware.** Prevent trash from entering the water. It is a hazard to cetaceans and other forms of wildlife.

• **Follow local regulations and guidelines for wildlife watching.** Different rules apply in different places and it is the responsibility of you and your boat operator to know what they are and follow them. Whale-watching regulators are now restricting the number of operators that can view cetaceans at a given time, limiting watching time (e.g., to a third of daylight hours) and defining refuge areas in which cetaceans cannot be approached. If you experience operators flouting the rules, let the relevant authorities know.

CHOOSING AN OPERATOR

Reputable whale-watching operators follow good practice and put the welfare of cetaceans first. When planning a whale-watching trip, find out which local whale-watching operators are recommended by wildlife or whale conservation organisations. For how long have they been operating? Do they have a good safety record? Do they have naturalists on board to explain what is happening? What is their success rate at finding whales? Do they have good working relationships with scientists and conservationists? What kinds of wildlife interaction can you expect? Only by asking such questions can you be sure that your whale-watching provider will put the welfare of the animals first, while ensuring you have the best opportunity of seeing their natural behaviour in the wild, and in relative safety.

Below: A humpback whale breaching close to a whale-watching boat in Hervey Bay, Queensland, Australia.

Where to Watch

There are many choices when it comes to deciding which cetaceans to watch and how to watch them. You can fly over eastern Australian waters in a light aircraft to search for humpback whales, or kayak in Greenland to look for belugas. In Monkey Mia, Western Australia, you can stand in the shallows with wild dolphins, and off the Dominican Republic you can snorkel in the water while humpback whales rise around you. Boat tours run from half-day excursions to several-week expeditions. Whichever whale-watching experience you seek, you will need to plan ahead so that you are in the right place at the right time, and with the right operator.

SHALLOW-WATER SPECIES

Many cetacean species favour shallow waters. Shallow waters lie above continental shelves – the submerged edges of continents – and, in most cases, they are no deeper than about 200 m (650 ft). You can see shallow-water species from the shore or on short boat trips.

Some medium-sized baleen whales, such as grey, humpback and right whales, migrate near or along coastlines in a fairly predictable manner year after year, and it is not difficult to plan to be there at the right time. Porpoises and many dolphin species stay in coastal waters year round, although their precise locations often shift with the seasons. Belugas and narwhals of arctic and subarctic waters are two of the world's most unusual species that frequent shallow waters.

DEEP-WATER SPECIES

Deep-water species prefer the waters beyond continental shelves where the seabed drops to about 4 km (2.5 miles) in depth, but can plunge to more than double this in the world's deepest trenches. Deep water lies close to shore alongside oceanic islands that are far from continents.

Species you can see in deep water include sperm, pilot and most rorqual whales. Beaked whales are often found where there are steep slopes in the sea, such as alongside submerged dormant volcanoes. Far from continents, oceanic forms of common, bottlenose and other dolphins gather in large schools. Some of the most interesting discoveries – identifying a new beaked whale species or finding out more about little-known dwarf and pygmy sperm whales – await those who venture over deep water.

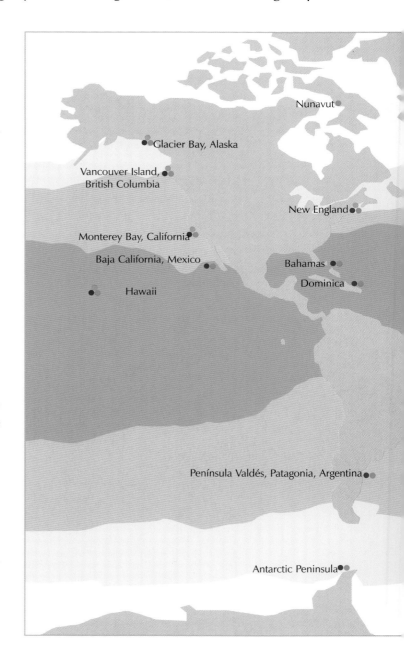

21 GREAT PLACES IN THE WORLD WHERE YOU CAN SEE CETACEANS

Where a particular species can be found depends on where its food is located; where water is of suitable quality, temperature and depth; and where the animal is less likely to be disturbed by predators or people. To be in the right place at the right time, learn a species' needs and be aware of how populations move with the seasons.

CLIMATE ZONES
- Tropical and subtropical
- Warm temperate
- Cold temperate
- Subarctic, arctic/subantarctic, antarctic
- Permanent ice

WHAT YOU CAN SEE
- whales
- dolphins
- porpoises

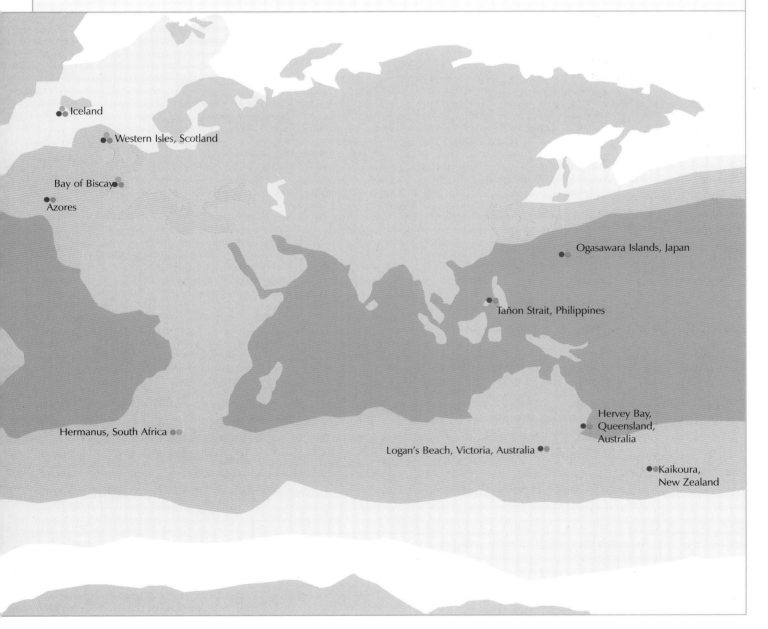

DAY TRIPS

According to whale expert Erich Hoyt, who surveyed whale watching across the world for a major report in 2001, more than two-thirds of whale watching is done from a boat. Many of these trips are of a day's duration or less, during which vessels go to specific locations near the coast where the chances of encountering whales, dolphins or porpoises are high. Motorised vessels range from those that take fewer than a dozen people to those that carry hundreds. Usually, there is a guide on board – often an employed naturalist – who provides background information and narrates what is happening when any cetacean is encountered.

There are also opportunities for land-based day trips. Off many major landmasses and offshore islands there are excellent opportunities for seeing cetaceans from the shore. Land-based whale watching is most highly developed in Australia, Canada, South Africa and the United States, but many offshore islands, such as the Azores, the Canaries, the Hawaiian Islands and Iceland, provide excellent land-based opportunities. In many locations there are purpose-built platforms for whale watching with display boards explaining what you can observe. In the Azores, lookout towers that were once used by whalers now have a more benign use as vantage points for whale watchers.

WHALE-WATCHING CRUISES

The range of opportunities for seeing cetaceans on longer trips, whether you are taking a four-week cruise to Antarctica and the Southern Ocean or launching a kayak from a shore camp in Baja California to see grey whales, is growing year by year. It is now possible to join cruise vessels going to arctic Russia to see bowhead whales, narwhals and belugas. Or you can work alongside a scientific team in the Bahamas, monitoring the activities of local populations of dolphins and beaked whales. Many whale-conservation organisations now run longer whale-watching trips, with narration provided by world-class cetacean experts who can provide deep insight into the lives of the whales, dolphins and porpoises you encounter.

HELPING SCIENTISTS

By going on well-organised whale-watching trips, you can greatly help scientists who are researching cetacean behaviour. Even on a one-day trip, you can be of real help to naturalists on board as an 'extra pair of eyes' scanning the horizon. Increasingly, commercial whale-watching trips chronicle their daily observations in a very systematic way, recording the location of the encounter using GPS (global positioning system), documenting behaviour, and seeking to identify the species or even the precise individuals involved. Photo-identification libraries exist for thousands of humpback and killer whales, and by taking photographs or video with a digital camera, you can become an 'extra camera lens'. By paying to go on whale-watching trips, you are also supporting ongoing research financially.

CLOSE ENCOUNTERS

In some parts of the world it is possible to get within touching distance of cetaceans, such as by 'swimming with dolphins'. Normal practice is not to touch a cetacean, for several good reasons. Hands can transfer grease to the cetacean's skin, altering its protective surface properties. Infections can be passed from human to animal through the air or by contact. There are also real physical dangers in getting close to such powerful creatures, even if they do not wish you any harm. An accidental tail swipe from a whale could easily crush you. Very occasionally, people are killed or injured when cetaceans feel threatened. In Baja California in the 1990s, two men were killed by a grey whale when their boat elbowed its way between her and her calf. In Brazil in 1994, a man was head-butted and killed by a dolphin after he tried to push objects down its blowhole – an action that is life-threatening to any cetacean.

On the other hand, there are some documented cases of dolphins having helped rescue people. In 1996, for example, a shark attacked American Martin Richardson while he was swimming in the Red Sea. According to Martin's rescuers, when they arrived three dolphins had surrounded Martin and were fin-slapping and lobtailing, helping to keep the shark at bay.

Do have a close encounter with a cetacean . . . but not too close. Good practice when whale watching is about the welfare of both you and the animal.

Right: Two Atlantic spotted dolphins swimming close to a snorkeller in the Bahamas.

Conservation

Of the 86 or so species of cetacean, at least 10 are classified as endangered and some are likely to become extinct in the next few decades unless preventive action is taken. Since the moratorium on commercial whaling in 1986, the hunting of whales has declined greatly but has not stopped entirely. Several countries still capture whales, dolphins and porpoises for meat, oil and other products. And many animals drown accidentally, caught in nets set for fish. Since the 1950s, pollution and habitat alteration – the modification of the places where animals live – have become major threats to shallow-water species. As the global climate changes, shifts in ocean currents will also have unpredictable consequences for many cetacean species.

CHANGING ATTITUDES

By the 1980s, industrial whaling had devastated the populations of larger whales. More than two million whales were killed in the Southern Hemisphere in the 20th century. By the 1960s the world's blue whale population had declined by more than 90%. Our attitudes to cetaceans have changed remarkably in the past 50 years as scientists and wildlife campaigners have generated public awareness of our kinship with whales, dolphins and porpoises. Industrial whaling, where an explosive harpoon is fired into the side of a whale and it slowly dies of shock, exhaustion and blood loss, has come to be seen by most people as barbaric.

CURRENT THREATS

Whaling on a large scale may have stopped (at least temporarily), but cetaceans – particularly those that frequent coastal waters and freshwater – are still vulnerable to pollution and habitat alteration. Toothed whales are particularly susceptible to pollution because they lie at or near the top of food chains. Contaminants accumulate inside living organisms and become concentrated as they pass from one animal to the next through food chains. Toothed whales that feed on fish, squid and other marine mammals are likely to carry the highest pollutant loads. The population of belugas living in the St Lawrence River between the United States and Canada is down to about 10% of its numbers compared to 50 years ago, and the main culprit is probably pollution. The carcasses of dead whales have such high levels of pollutants that they are classed as toxic waste and have to be disposed of with great care.

Across the world, sea grass beds and mangrove forests, nursery grounds for fish and crustaceans that many toothed whales feed upon, are being destroyed to make way for shoreline developments ranging from fish farms to marinas, resorts and coastal industrial complexes. At the same time, new developments create more human interference, including noise and boat traffic, along with changes in the chemical quality of coastal waters. Coastal cetaceans are forced to move on.

Fishing nets also pose a danger to cetaceans. In 1992, international laws banned the use of drift nets – nets of mesh many miles long that hang in the ocean and catch animals indiscriminately. Nevertheless, such nets are still used illegally. Other forms of net can take small cetaceans by accident – so-called bycatch. New technologies and better fishing practices are reducing the toll on cetaceans, but implementation needs to be accelerated. The impact of overfishing by humans on cetaceans should also be addressed. Overfishing has devastated many of the world's fish populations, to the detriment of those cetaceans that compete for them.

WHAT YOU CAN DO

There is plenty that you can do to help stop the human-related activities that threaten cetaceans today. You can join wildlife organisations that campaign and take action to make the oceans cleaner, halt the destruction of coastal habitats and curb the over-exploitation of marine stocks. You can help persuade your local and national politicians to make such issues a high priority. When you go whale watching, choose to use the best operators that support wildlife organisations and scientists and that apply best

Above: A juvenile sperm whale stranded near Hong Kong in 2003. The animal could not be rehabilitated and was put down humanely by a vet.

practice. Observe good practice yourself, by not chasing, feeding or touching animals, and insist that others behave with similar respect. You can support 'dolphin-safe' campaigns and check with your food suppliers about where your marine produce comes from. Has it been caught or farmed in a way that is sustainable? You can visit sealife centres and find out what they are doing to encourage good practice. If they keep cetaceans, when are they planning to return them to the wild? If they have no such plans, why not? Finally, keep yourself informed. At the back of this book is a list of publications and websites where you can find out more.

STRANDING

Each year, thousands of cetaceans strand along shorelines. Deep-water species, such as pilot, sperm and false killer whales, are common victims, but most species strand at one time or another. In some cases, strandings occur because animals have misinterpreted the contours of the seabed and have accidentally run aground. In other cases, an individual may be disoriented because of an illness or injury that has affected the animal's hearing and, in turn, its ability to echolocate.

What should you do if you find a stranded whale or a whale in distress? Contact the Coast Guard, local police or relevant wildlife agency and they will bring in whale experts, including vets, to assess the situation. Avoid touching or moving the animal, as this could do more harm than good. In strandings of schools of smaller cetaceans, some animals might be able to be successfully refloated. However, in many cases an individual strands because it is unwell and near death. In January 2006, an immature northern bottlenose whale made its way up the River Thames into central London and beached itself. This deep-water species was several hundred miles from its normal habitat. Its very presence there, and its subsequent behaviour, suggested it was ailing. Despite the best efforts of a rescue team, it died while being transported out to sea.

Identification

It is the sudden appearance of a whale, dolphin or porpoise at the sea surface that provides the thrill of any whale-watching trip. Identifying the species of the animal you are viewing is not always easy. Rough seas or bright sunshine create tricky viewing conditions. Identifying any cetacean is a gradual process of elimination, ticking off items from a checklist of features. It is common even for cetacean experts to come back from a trip with 'unidentified species' written in their notebooks. But, with experience, you can learn what to look for and become adept at spotting the telltale combinations of shape, size, colour and behaviour that enable you to distinguish one species from another.

BLOW CHARACTERISTICS

The blow, or spout, the whale's moisture-rich outbreath, can be useful for identifying large whales. On a calm day, the height, shape and prominence of the blow can be a vital identifying clue. However, interpreting blow characteristics, as with any other identification feature, needs to be treated with care. The blow when an exhausted whale surfaces after a long dive is likely to be taller than when it is swimming slowly at the surface. In a strong wind, the blow of a baleen whale could be mistaken for that of a sperm whale, which produces a blow angled forward and to one side.

Below: The blow of a humpback whale – distinct, tall and bushy.

WATCHING CHECKLIST

Identifying any cetacean is a process of elimination. Once you have narrowed down options based on location and habitat, one feature is rarely enough for a positive identification. Gather as much information as possible before coming to a conclusion. Be unsure rather than make a misidentification based on guessing. There are 12 points to consider.

1. Geographical location and habitat, such as coast or river.
2. Size. Try comparing to the length of the boat.
3. Unusual features, such as a tusk.
4. The shape and markings of the flukes (tail).
5. Dorsal fin size, shape and position.
6. Flipper (pectoral fin) size, shape and position.
7. Head size, shape and colour. Whether beak present or not.
8. Body shape, colour and markings.
9. Blow characteristics (larger species only).
10. Group size, or number of individuals travelling together.
11. Surface behaviour, such as breaching or lobtailing.
12. Dive sequence, from surfacing to disappearance.

Above: A large group of spinner dolphins porpoising off Hawaii.

GROUP SIZE

The number of animals you can see together is a useful species indicator. Some species – such as pilot whales and some oceanic dolphins – gather in large numbers at certain times. Many species, however, live in small groups, and some, such as bowhead whales, may be solitary for some of the time. Be aware that all members of a group may not surface at the same time, so many more could be beneath the surface. Only by observing the group for many minutes may you be able to make an estimate of group size.

BODY SHAPE, SIZE AND COLOUR

It is difficult to estimate the size of an animal unless there is a reference feature, such as the length of a boat or the height of a buoy. However, even estimating that the cetacean is large (more than 10 m or 33 ft long), of medium size (3 to 10 m, or 10 to 33 ft) or small (less than 3 m or 10 ft) is a quick way of narrowing the range of possibilities. The animal's overall body shape, such as whether it is bulky or sleek, can be a useful clue, although many cetaceans do not reveal enough of themselves to give a reliable impression. The observed colour of an animal varies greatly with water clarity and lighting conditions, and an animal will appear dark if you are facing the sun when viewing it. The best diagnostic features are bold markings or contrasts in tone, as are found on the flanks of some dolphins and porpoises.

HOW TO USE THIS BOOK

The following symbols are used throughout. A symbol that is highlighted in red indicates that it is a useful identification feature.

 Fluking behaviour and the shape, size and colour of flukes.

 The height, shape, colour or position of the dorsal fin.

 Flipper size, shape, colour or position.

 The shape of the head and any distinctive features such as colour, markings or tusks.

 Body size and shape and any distinctive features such as colour or markings.

 The height, shape and visibility of the blow (larger cetaceans only).

 Group size. This may include a range of possibilities for different activities.

 Common surface behaviour and the typical dive sequence.

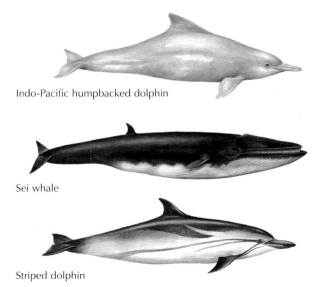

Indo-Pacific humpbacked dolphin

Sei whale

Striped dolphin

HEAD SHAPE AND COLOUR

Getting a clear view of the side of the animal's head is one of the best ways to identify it. Among baleen whales, for example, all rorqual whales (except the humpback) have a pointed snout in profile, while right whales (except the pygmy) and other baleen whales have blunter snouts.

Among oceanic dolphins and some other toothed whales, deciding whether the animal has an obvious beak or not narrows the options quickly. Bold head markings, and the position of tusks in males, help distinguish the various species of beaked whale. The shape and size of the forehead, or melon, is another useful diagnostic feature.

DIVE SEQUENCE AND FLUKING

The manner in which a cetacean breaks the surface to breathe, and then dives again, is called its dive sequence. This can be quite distinctive for a given species. Whether an animal is simply travelling from one place to another, or is staying in the vicinity and deep-diving for food, changes the nature of its dive sequence. At the start of a dive, an animal may raise its flukes high into the air ('flukes up') or not ('flukes down'), providing a distinguishing feature. Finally, the shape of the flukes can vary markedly between species. The colour and markings on the flukes, and whether they have a notch in the middle of concave, convex or straight trailing edges, are well worth noting.

Below: Two humpback whales both raising a flipper. Notice the knobs on the flippers' leading edges and their pale markings.

DORSAL FIN SHAPE AND SIZE

Most cetaceans have a dorsal fin, and its shape, size and position can be useful diagnostic features. Carefully record the fin's relative height and its shape. Are the leading and trailing edges curved or straight? If curved, are they convex (bulging outward) or concave (curving inward)? Is the fin tip pointed or rounded? Is the base broad or narrow? The fin's position on the body can also be a sound identification feature.

FLIPPER SHAPE AND SIZE

Unless the animal breaches, leaps, spyhops or flipper-slaps, the flippers may not become visible. Recording their relative size and their shape, colour, markings and position can help identify the species. In some species, such as the humpback whale and pilot whales, flipper shape is very distinctive.

SURFACE BEHAVIOUR

Various types of surface behaviour – breaching, leaping, porpoising, flipper-slapping, lobtailing, logging, spyhopping and so on – are more common in some species than in others, and the way an animal performs such behaviours can be diagnostic. Minke whales, for example, tend to breach at a shallow angle. Spinner dolphins commonly spin when they leap.

HEAD SHAPE

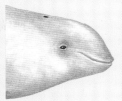

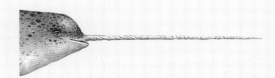

The beak of the Ganges dolphin can be as long as 45 cm (18 in).

A beluga has a blunt head with a rounded forehead (melon). The beak is absent or very short.

The narwhal has a bulbous melon and little or no beak. Adult males have a prominent forward-pointing tusk.

DORSAL FIN SHAPE

Killer whales have a very tall dorsal fin, especially in males.

The pygmy sperm whale has a small, hooked dorsal fin.

The common dolphin's dorsal fin has a nearly pointed tip and a concave trailing edge.

FLIPPER SHAPE

The flippers of pilot whales are long and narrow with a distinct bulge on the leading edge.

Killer whale flippers are unusually broad and rounded.

The flippers of a humpback are extremely long, with a knobbly leading edge and rounded tips.

FLUKES SHAPE

The flukes of a finless porpoise have smooth, concave trailing edges and a deep notch in the middle.

A sperm whale's flukes are broad and triangular with an almost straight trailing edge.

Bowhead whales have fairly narrow flukes with pointed tips and concave trailing edges.

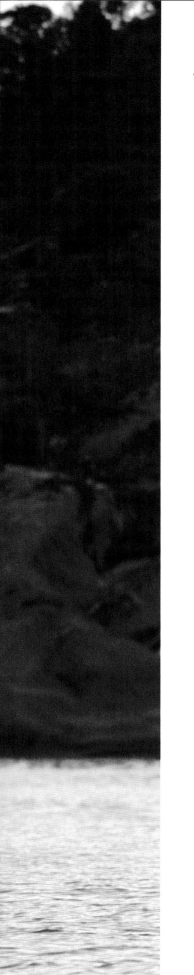

Watching Whales, Dolphins and Porpoises

Whale watching, whether you are close to home or in a far-off exotic location, can be an inspiring and unforgettable adventure. With more than 85 species of cetaceans in the world, from dolphins that weigh less than the average person to baleen whales that weigh 1,000 times that, there is something to excite everyone's curiosity. But to make the most of your whale-watching experience, it is important to know the basics: where and when to go, and what to look for.

The pages that follow introduce you to particular groups of cetaceans, describing various species together according to their taxonomic similarity – that is, how closely related they are in evolutionary terms – and how similar they appear when observed in the wild. For example, oceanic dolphins are covered in two sections: those that have prominent beaks and those that do not. Detailed illustrations highlight the key physical features of each group, and every species that can be found within that group is listed. In this manner, all the world's cetaceans are identified and compared.

We then examine more closely those species that you are likely to see on organised whale-watching trips. For each of these species, you will learn its most recognisable features, its geographical range, aspects of its natural history and the places in the world where you are most likely to observe it in the wild.

Although you can see cetaceans from the shore in many places, more often than not whale watching involves going out in a boat. When choosing a whale-watching operator, do so with care, for your own safety and for that of the animals you are watching.

Left: A killer whale spyhopping in Tysfjord, Norway.

Watching Rorqual Whales

Rorqual whales are the largest family of baleen whales, both in number of species and average length of individuals. Rorquals include some of the most spectacular and acrobatic of all whales. The name rorqual comes from *rorhval*, Norwegian for 'furrow', and refers to the numerous grooves or pleats in the throat of rorqual whales. These allow the throat to bulge out like an expanding concertina as the whale takes in a mouthful of water when filter-feeding. Rorqual whales range in length from the minke whale, at up to 10.5 m (35 ft) long, to the blue whale, which can attain 30 m (99 ft). Since 2003, scientists have added at least two species of rorqual whale to the traditional list of six.

IDENTIFICATION

All rorqual whales, with the exception of the humpback, have a sleek body shape and a relatively pointed snout in profile. This combination distinguishes rorquals from other large whales, such as right whales, the grey whale and sperm whales. Only the pygmy right whale has a snout that could be mistaken for that of a rorqual.

In rorquals the head is broad when viewed from above. The forehead is gently sloping, almost flat, and along it, visible at close range, runs a central ridge (in Bryde's whale, three ridges). The ridge ends at a splash-guard, which is a hump just in front of the two blowholes.

The feature by which rorquals gain their name – the throat furrows – are visible only at fairly close range when the whale turns on its side or back, or when it breaches. Rorquals have more numerous and prominent throat grooves than any other species. The humpback whale, with 12 to 36, has the fewest grooves among rorquals, while fin whales have up to about 100.

Below: The sei whale, a medium-sized rorqual, showing the major physical features characteristic of all.

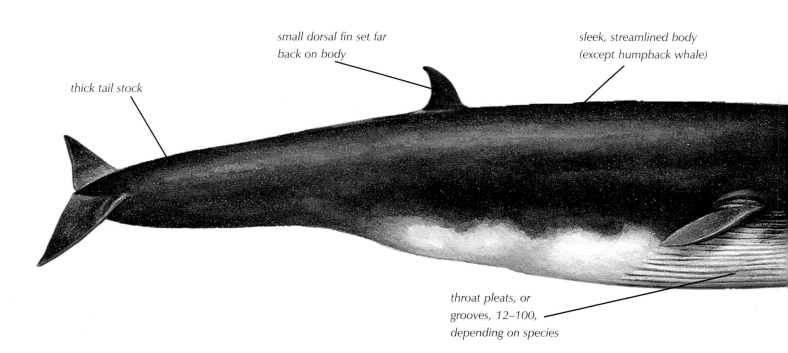

small dorsal fin set far back on body

sleek, streamlined body (except humpback whale)

thick tail stock

throat pleats, or grooves, 12–100, depending on species

FEEDING

Most rorquals feed by lunging, with mouth agape, at gatherings of small prey, such as fish, krill or squid. Sei whales sometimes skim-feed, that is, swim along fairly steadily near the sea surface, feeding more or less continuously. A rorqual's throat pleats allow the throat to expand enormously to take in seawater laden with food items. An adult blue whale consumes several tonnes of food each day – made up of millions of krill – and to do so the whale has to filter many thousands of tonnes of water.

Above: A humpback feeding in Frederick Sound, Alaska, where they are watchable from April to July. The whale's throat pleats are clearly visible.

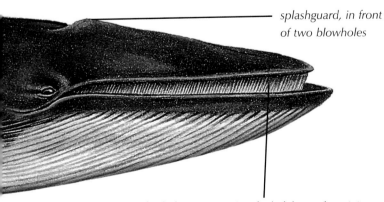

splashguard, in front of two blowholes

the baleen, a curtain of whalebone (keratin) strands that the whale uses to strain fish, squid or crustaceans from seawater

RORQUAL WHALES

BLUE WHALE
Huge body. Dark blue-grey back, mottled with pale grey. Dorsal fin small and set far back.

FIN WHALE
Large body. Dark grey back without mottling. Dorsal fin more prominent than in blue whale.

HUMPBACK WHALE
Dark grey or black body. Knobbly head. Flippers huge and at least partly white. Flukes raised high on diving.

SEI WHALE
Similar to fin whale but smaller. Dorsal fin tall and sickle shaped. Blow vertical.

BRYDE'S WHALE
Similar to sei whale but smaller. Has three lengthwise ridges on upper head (all other rorquals have one).

MINKE WHALE
Sleek with pointed snout. Often, white band on flipper. Snout surfaces first. Strongly arches its tail stock on diving.

Blue Whale

The blue whale, which is actually a mottled blue-grey, is the largest animal on Earth. Its heart is the size of a small car and an average adult person could fit inside its largest blood vessels. In the heyday of whaling, in the first half of the 20th century, whalers caught some specimens that were 33 m (108 ft) long and weighed about 200 tonnes. Today, following intensive hunting until the 1960s, blue whales tend to be slightly smaller and the world population has shrunk to less than 5% of its original number.

The 10,000 or so blue whales that remain are scattered widely and patchily across the world's oceans. In summer, most blue whales feed in polar and cool temperate regions, where nutrient-rich waters support a vast population of phytoplankton (microscopic algae) on which krill, the whale's prey, feed. In winter, the whales migrate to tropical and subtropical waters to breed, usually staying well away from coastlines. In a few locations, such as off the coast of California and western Mexico, blue whales may be resident all year round.

Above: The flukes of a blue whale diving in the Gulf of California (Sea of Cortez), Mexico. Blue whales are watchable here January to April.

WHERE TO WATCH

Watching choice: West coast of the United States and Mexico.
When to go: August to October off California, Oregon and Washington. January to April in the Gulf of California off southern California and Mexico.
Getting there: Many of the coastal resorts offer whale-watching trips. Major transport hubs include Seattle, San Francisco, Los Angeles and Mexico City.

☐ Ocean	■ Known range	☐ Permanent ice

FACTFILE

Scientific name: *Balaenoptera musculus*
Family: Balaenopteridae
Range: All oceans
Habitat: Oceanic waters
Status: Endangered
Population: Probably 8,000–12,000
Diet: Crustaceans, especially krill; occasionally squid
Length: 23–30 m (75–99 ft); females larger than males
Weight: 100–130 tonnes

IDENTIFICATION

 Flukes are occasionally raised before a dive. Tail stock is very thick. Flukes are elongate with a slight notch in the middle.

 Dorsal fin is stubby and set far back on the body. Less prominent than on fin whales.

 Flippers are blue-grey. Long and slender.

Head is broad and flattened. Narrow in profile. Large splashguard.

 Streamlined body is extremely long. Back and flanks are dark bluish grey, mottled with paler grey blotches. Underside is white or pale blue-grey.

 Tall, narrow blow up to 10 m (33 ft) high.

 Usually found singly or in pairs, with larger groups at good feeding grounds.

 Approachable, but swims rapidly if disturbed. Youngsters breach, but adults only rarely. When undisturbed, dives of 5–20 minutes may be followed by 12–18 blows at 10- to 20-second intervals.

IDENTIFICATION

 Arches tail stock before a dive, rarely exposing flukes. Central ridge runs along the top of the thick tail stock. Flukes are elongate with a distinct notch in the middle.

 Dorsal fin is backward sloping and set about three-quarters back along the body.

 Flippers are dark grey above and pale below. Slender and moderately long.

 Head is broad and flattened. Narrow in profile. Right side paler than left.

 Streamlined body is long. Back and flanks are dark grey without mottling. Underside is pale.

 Tall, narrow blow up to 8 m (26 ft) high, which takes several seconds to dissipate.

 Usually found singly, in pairs or in small pods, but large groups of up to 100 at good feeding grounds.

 Fast swimming and approachable, but difficult to track. Sometimes breach or lunge-feed, exposing the pale side of the head. When undisturbed, dives of 5–15 minutes are usually followed by 2–5 blows at 10- to 20-second intervals.

Fin Whale

The fin whale is second in size only to the blue whale. It is sometimes called the finback, or razorback, because of the ridge that runs along the upper side of the tail stock. The species is unusual in having different pigmentation on the right and left sides of the head. The right side is paler, both inside and outside the mouth. This feature is probably linked to feeding. The fin whale is sometimes visible lunging across the water surface, turning its head to one side as it does so. The flash of white may serve to scare a school of fish into a tight ball, making it easier for the whale to consume them.

In the 19th and 20th centuries whalers heavily hunted this sleek, fast-swimming whale, although its numbers still remain much greater than those of the blue whale. Fin whales are quite social and it is common to find them in pods of three to seven individuals. Most fin whales migrate to polar and temperate waters in summer to feed, taking advantage of abundant krill and small schooling fish. In winter, many migrate to tropical or subtropical waters to mate and calve. Others prefer to stay in cooler waters throughout the year.

Above: The backward-sloping dorsal fin of a fin whale in the Gulf of California, Mexico, where fin whales are watchable January to April.

FACTFILE

Scientific name: *Balaenoptera physalus*
Family: Balaenopteridae
Range: All oceans
Habitat: Oceanic waters
Status: Classed as endangered, but locally common
Population: More than 100,000
Diet: Schooling fish and crustaceans; occasionally squid
Length: 18–26 m (59–85 ft); females larger than males
Weight: 30–80 tonnes

WHERE TO WATCH

Watching choice: New England, on the east coast of the United States.
When to go: April to October off Maine, New Hampshire and Massachusetts.
Getting there: More than 30 whale-watching companies operate from at least 17 coastal communities. Boston is the main regional transport hub.

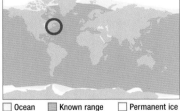

☐ Ocean ■ Known range ☐ Permanent ice

Humpback Whale

FACTFILE

Scientific name: *Megaptera novaeangliae*
Family: Balaenopteridae
Range: All oceans
Habitat: Oceanic and coastal waters
Status: Vulnerable
Population: 20,000–30,000
Diet: Krill and schooling fish
Length: 12–16 m (40–53 ft); females larger than males
Weight: 25–35 tonnes

IDENTIFICATION

 Flukes are raised high before a dive. Distinct notch in the middle and ragged trailing edges. Pale markings on underside are distinctive.

 Dorsal fin is located about two-thirds back along the body. Low and stubby.

 Flippers are very large and round-ended. Ranging from black to pale above. Pale below.

 Head is broad with knobs (tubercles) on top and on the lower jaw.

 Bulky body with a black to dark grey upper side and flanks, and a partially white underside.

 Distinctive bushy blow up to 3 m (10 ft) high.

 Family groups of up to 3 or 4, with larger groups at feeding and breeding grounds.

 Slow swimming. Not afraid of boats and often inquisitive. Frequently spyhops. May breach, lobtail and flipper-slap several times in a row. May lie on its back with flippers in the air. When undisturbed, dives of 3–9 minutes may be followed by 4–8 blows at 15- to 30-second intervals.

The humpback whale is the third-largest rorqual species by weight but the fourth longest, being slightly shorter on average than the sei whale. The humpback is the most distinctive rorqual of all, with its stocky body, knobbly head and above all, its enormous, round-ended, pale-marked flippers. When the whale dives, it raises its flukes high in the air, and the pale markings on the underside are obvious. The shape of the flukes and the colour and pattern of the underside are as distinctive as fingerprints, and scientists and whale watchers alike photograph them to identify individual whales. Several thousand whales are now on record.

The humpback is distinct from other rorquals to the extent that it is placed in a separate genus. Its scientific name, *Megaptera novaeangliae*, means 'big-winged New Englander', in reference to its flippers and the place where it was first described scientifically.

The humpback is arguably the most exciting whale to watch. It is slow-moving and often cavorts around at the sea surface, breaching or lobtailing. Sometimes it will lie on its back and wave one or both flippers in the air. Occasionally it brings a flipper down with a crash.

In the winter breeding season in warm latitudes, adult males chase after females and hang almost

WHERE TO WATCH

Watching choice: East coast of Australia.
When to go: Humpbacks are watchable on the northward and southward leg of their

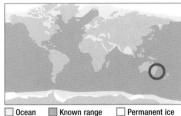

☐ Ocean ■ Known range ☐ Permanent ice

migration and at their spawning and calving grounds. New South Wales in late May to July and late September to November. Queensland in August to November.
Getting there: Whale-watching trips go from Byron Bay, Coff's Harbour, Eden, Fairy Meadow and Wollongong in New South Wales; Airlie Beach, Bundaberg, Hervey Bay and Tangalooma in Queensland. Brisbane and Sydney are the main regional transport hubs.

Left: A young humpback whale breaching in Frederick Sound, Alaska. Notice the barnacles growing on the chin and flippers.

Left: Humpback whales surfacing to engulf bubble-netted fish. The baleen is clearly visible in the mouth of the whale in the foreground.

MIGRATIONS

The migrations of humpbacks are, along with those of grey whales, the longest of any marine mammal. The longest record goes to one stock of humpbacks that migrates between the Southern Ocean and Colombian waters, covering some 19,000 km (12,000 miles) annually in a round trip. There are at least eight distinct populations of humpback whales in the Southern Hemisphere and about the same number in the Northern. Because winter is roughly between November and February in the Northern Hemisphere but around June to August in the Southern, the stocks in the two hemispheres do not meet and intermingle. There is also a population of humpbacks in the Arabian Sea that appears to stay in the same locality the whole year round.

Southern Hemisphere humpbacks tend to eat mostly krill, while Northern Hemisphere humpbacks also take schooling fish such as herring and capelin.

BUBBLE-NETTING

Humpbacks employ some of the most extraordinary feeding techniques of any cetacean. Humpbacks will engulf a bait ball of fish by direct attack, or may slap

motionless in the water 'singing' complex songs that warn off males and attract females.

Being fairly large, slow-moving whales that often inhabit coastal waters and follow regular migration routes, humpbacks were favoured and easy prey for whalers. Between the 18th and late 20th centuries, the world population of humpbacks probably fell by more than 90%. Since 1966 the species has been protected (although illegal catches by Soviet vessels took place in the 1970s). The humpback is one of the few cetaceans that is making a reasonable comeback after intensive exploitation. Numbers have probably risen from about 10,000 to more than 20,000 in the last 40 years.

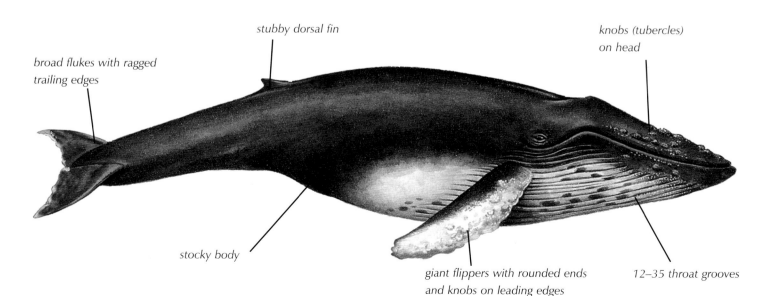

broad flukes with ragged trailing edges

stubby dorsal fin

knobs (tubercles) on head

stocky body

giant flippers with rounded ends and knobs on leading edges

12–35 throat grooves

Above: The underside of the flukes of a humpback whale. The shape and colour pattern are unique to each whale.

the water nearby, sending shockwaves that temporarily stun the fish, allowing the whale to swallow them with ease.

Bubble-net fishing is the whale's most inventive technique. Some groups of whales swim rapidly in circles around and below a school of fish or a swarm of krill. As they do so the whales blow bubbles out of their blowholes, creating a curtain of bubbles surrounding the prey. The group gradually tightens the circle and spirals upward, forcing the school or swarm toward the surface. Finally, the whales rise in unison with mouths agape to engulf the tightly packed prey. Up to 20 whales may work together in this remarkable example of cooperative hunting. They even vary the size of the bubbles according to the size of the prey: large bubbles for herring and smaller bubbles for krill. It is an astonishing sight to watch a dozen or more humpbacks set their bubble-net trap and then rise through the water with their mouths agape while hundreds of fish scatter for their lives.

SINGING

Male humpbacks sing the most extraordinarily complex songs of any mammal, except humans. In the breeding season, adult male humpbacks hang almost vertically in the water, head down, and sing. The song is a complex composition of grunts, whistles, chirps, squeals and wails arranged in a number of themes. The songs last from a few minutes to as long as half an hour. After a short respite to catch its breath, the whale repeats the song. This can go on for many hours, day and night.

What do the songs mean? We don't exactly know, although they coincide with courtship and breeding, which means they are probably used by males to court females and to intimidate rival males. But they may have other functions, too. Intriguingly, males in the same population sing songs that are similar, and these songs gradually evolve over the months and years. Males in separate populations sing different compositions. A humpback whale expert, hearing a song recording, can tell which population the whale came from and when the recording was made.

Sei Whale

The sei (pronounced 'say') whale is the third-longest rorqual whale but the fourth largest by weight. It is much more streamlined than the humpback whale. The sei's name comes from the Norwegian *seje*, meaning pollack (coalfish), a member of the cod family. In Norwegian waters, sei whales often feed on pollack, hence the fish and the whale have become associated.

This medium-sized whale is easily confused with the fin whale and especially Bryde's whale. It can be distinguished from Bryde's by its dorsal fin, set farther forward on the body, and its dive sequence, which does not involve arching the tail stock. Seen at close range, a Bryde's whale has three ridges running along its head, while a sei has only one. Although the distributions of sei and Bryde's whales overlap in warmer waters, the sei travels into cooler waters as far as latitude 60°N and 60°S. Bryde's whales stay in warmer waters and rarely venture much beyond 40°N or 40°S.

Sei whales migrate between cool-water summer feeding grounds and warm-water winter breeding grounds. They tend to stay in deeper water and are rarely seen near coasts.

Above: A sei whale calf underwater in the Azores, North Atlantic Ocean, where seis are occasionally encountered between April and October.

WHERE TO WATCH

Watching choice: Cruise ships to Antarctica.
When to go: Late November to March.
Getting there: Cruise ships leave from ports in Australia, New Zealand

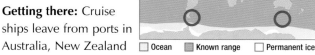

Ocean ☐ Known range ■ Permanent ice ☐

and South Africa, but especially Argentina and Chile in South America. There are opportunities to see many other cetaceans on the trip, including orcas, other rorqual whales and Southern Hemisphere species such as the southern bottlenose whale.

FACTFILE

Scientific name: *Balaenoptera borealis*
Family: Balaenopteridae
Range: All oceans but not far into polar oceans
Habitat: Oceanic waters
Status: Locally common, but classified as endangered
Population: Fewer than 60,000
Diet: Schooling fish, crustaceans and squid
Length: 13–21 m (43–69 ft); females larger than males
Weight: 20–30 tonnes

IDENTIFICATION

 Does not arch its tail stock before diving. Does not expose its flukes. Flukes are elongate with a distinct notch in the middle.

 Upright dorsal fin with arched trailing edge is set about three-fifths back along the body.

 Flippers are dark grey above and below. Slender and moderately long.

 Head is broad and flattened. Narrow in profile. Both sides of head are the same colour.

 Streamlined body is long. Back is dark or bluish grey. Underside is white or pale grey.

 Tall, narrow blow up to 3 m (10 ft) high.

 Found singly, in pairs, or in small pods, but up to 50 on good feeding grounds.

 Fast swimming, they sometimes skim-feed just below the surface with only the dorsal fin visible and blow every 40–60 seconds. Surfacing from a dive, the blowhole and dorsal fin usually appear simultaneously. When undisturbed, dives of 5–20 minutes may be followed by 3–8 blows at 20- to 30-second intervals.

IDENTIFICATION

 Commonly arches its tail stock before diving. Does not raise its flukes. Flukes are elongate with a notch in middle.

 Prominent dorsal fin is set about three-quarters back along the body and has a very arched trailing edge.

 Flippers are slender and comparatively small. Smoky grey above and below.

 Head is broad and flattened. Narrow in profile. The top of the head has three parallel ridges (other rorqual whales have one).

 Streamlined body is long. Back and flanks are smoky grey. Underside ranges from white or pale yellow on throat to blue-grey or creamy grey near vent.

 Tall, narrow blow up to 4 m (13 ft) high.

 Found singly, in pairs, or in small pods of up to 7. As many as 30 may gather on good feeding grounds.

 A more erratic swimmer than the sei. At the surface, its sudden changes in direction are like those of a large dolphin. Can be very acrobatic, breaching near vertically several times in a row. When undisturbed, dives of 1–8 minutes are often followed by 4–7 blows.

Bryde's Whale

Bryde's (pronounced 'brood-ess') whale is strikingly similar to the sei whale, although slightly smaller, and it has three ridges on the top of the head instead of one. It was not until the early 1900s that whalers realised the two were distinct species. Bryde's whale gains its name from the Norwegian consul Johan Bryde, who helped set up a whaling station in Durban, South Africa, where the species was first described. Bryde's whale, unlike other rorqual whales, is conspicuously a warm-water species. It prefers water temperatures above 20°C (68°F), so it is most common between latitudes 30°N and 30°S.

Bryde's whale, because of its comparatively small size and lack of blubber, was not heavily exploited by whalers until the 1970s, so the population has been much less severely depleted than that of other rorqual whales, except the minke.

Scientists generally agree that Bryde's whale is at least two species: a larger, common form, *Balaenoptera brydei*, and a pygmy form called Eden's whale, *Balaenoptera edeni*. A third species, Omura's whale, *Balaenoptera omurai*, and possibly a fourth, may soon be recognised. The information given here relates to the common larger species.

Above: A Bryde's whale lunge-feeding on sardines off the east coast of South Africa. Note the three parallel ridges on top of the whale's head.

FACTFILE

Scientific name: *Balaenoptera brydei*
Family: Balaenopteridae
Range: Warmer Atlantic, Indian and Pacific oceans
Habitat: Oceanic waters
Status: Locally common
Population: Less than 100,000
Diet: Schooling fish and sometimes krill or copepods
Length: 12–15 m (39–50 ft); females larger than males
Weight: 12–20 tonnes

WHERE TO WATCH

Watching choice: Western Cape, South Africa.
When to go: July to September, when southern right whales are viewable from the shore and humpback whales are viewable offshore.

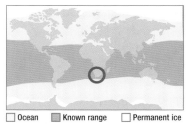

☐ Ocean ◼ Known range ☐ Permanent ice

Getting there: Boat-based whale-watching trips for Bryde's whales and other cetaceans operate from Hermanus, Gansbaai and Kleinbaai. The regional hub is Cape Town.

Minke Whale

The minke (pronounced 'mink-ey') whale – a lively, boldly marked whale – is the second smallest of all baleen whale species. Only the pygmy right whale, with which it can be confused, is smaller. Scientists have recently confirmed that the minke whale is at least two species: the northern minke whale (*Balaenoptera acutorostrata*) of the Northern Hemisphere and the southern minke whale (*Balaenoptera bonaerensis*) of the Southern. Their distributions overlap near the equator. There is also a dwarf form found in the Southern Hemisphere (not described here).

Taken together, the distribution of the two minke species is virtually oceanwide, from polar to tropical waters, with cooler waters preferred. Southern minke whales eat mainly krill, while northern minkes take schooling fish or copepods. Minke whales, because of their small size, have largely escaped heavy exploitation. Among baleen whales in general, and rorqual whales in particular, the northern minke is distinctive in having a white band on each flipper. Most southern minke whales lack this band. The dive sequence of both species is, however, distinctive, with the snout emerging first and the tail stock arching strongly before a dive.

Above: A southern minke whale near South Georgia, South Atlantic Ocean.

WHERE TO WATCH

Watching choice: West coast of Scotland and Western Isles.
When to go: April to October.
Getting there: Whale-watching tours, from a half-day to a week or more, operate variously from Dervaig (Isle of Mull), Gairloch, Mallaig and Oban. Glasgow and then Oban are the main regional transport hubs.

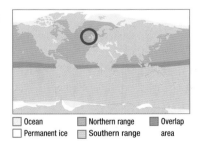

☐ Ocean   ▨ Northern range   ▨ Overlap
☐ Permanent ice   ▨ Southern range   area

FACTFILE

Scientific name: *Balaenoptera acutorostrata* (northern) and *Balaenoptera bonaerensis* (southern)
Family: Balaenopteridae
Range: All oceans, from polar to tropical regions
Habitat: Oceanic waters
Status: Common
Population: 500,000 to 1 million in total
Diet: Schooling fish or crustaceans (krill and copepods)
Length: 8–10.5 m (26–35 ft); females larger than males
Weight: 5–15 tonnes

IDENTIFICATION

 Strongly arches its tail stock before diving. Does not raise its flukes. Flukes are elongate with a slight notch in the middle. Underside tends to be paler than upper.

 Prominent dorsal fin is set about two-thirds back along the body and has an arched trailing edge.

 Flippers may have white band or pale markings above. Usually pale below. Slender and relatively short.

 Head is narrower than other rorqual whales and snout is more pointed. The top of the head has one ridge.

 Streamlined body. Back is black, dark grey or brown, with a broad pale or grey band extending up the middle flanks. Underside is white, pale grey or pale brown.

 Low, bushy, indistinct blow up to about 3 m (9 ft) high.

 Usually found singly, in pairs or in small pods. As many as 100 may gather in good feeding areas.

 Fast swimmer. Snout surfaces first. May suddenly appear alongside boat and just as quickly disappear. Occasionally spyhops. Breaches at an angle of 45° or less. When undisturbed, dives of 3–8 minutes are followed by 5–8 blows at less than 60-second intervals.

Watching Right and Grey Whales

The larger right whales are coastal species that swim slowly, float when dead and contain plentiful baleen (whalebone) and blubber. For these reasons, early whalers dubbed them the 'right' whales to hunt. The six species of right and grey whales are, like rorqual whales, all baleen whales. Their feeding apparatus is a series of frayed horny plates slung from the upper jaw. Right and grey whales have broad baleen plates. With the exception of the pygmy right whale, right and grey whales have more bulbous heads than rorquals, to accommodate the larger baleen. Between them, the six species inhabit the coastal regions of all oceans except the Southern Ocean. Two species are in danger of extinction.

IDENTIFICATION

Right and grey whales tend to be slower swimming than rorqual whales, and because they skim-feed at or near the surface, they are easier to observe. With the exception of the pygmy right whale, they have a narrow tail stock and no dorsal fin. They also lack the prominent throat grooves that are characteristic of rorqual whales. Grey whales have three to seven throat grooves, but they are much less obvious than those of rorquals.

Below: A grey whale, showing most of the major physical features characteristic of right whales as well.

FEEDING

Right whales and the bowhead whale skim-feed. They swim along with their mouth partly open so that water enters and suspended organisms become trapped on the baleen. The whale periodically closes its mouth and swallows the captured creatures. Grey whales are an exception and feed almost exclusively on the seabed. They suck up sediment rich in bottom-living organisms, and then expel the mud and water, trapping prey on the baleen.

absence of dorsal fin (but present in the pygmy right whale)

broad flukes

narrow tail stock (except in the pygmy right whale)

body stockier than most rorqual whales

PYGMY RIGHT WHALE

The pygmy right whale looks superficially like a rorqual but, with its down-curved mouth, large baleen and absence of throat pleats, it is more closely related to right whales. It reaches only about 6.5 m (21 ft) long – much smaller than other right whales. The pygmy right is found in the southern Atlantic, Indian and Pacific oceans, between about 31°S and 55°S. Confirmed sightings are rare. Its dive sequence, with the head and tail stock barely breaking the surface, is distinctive from that of the minke whale, but not easy to spot.

Above: Close-up of the baleen plates of a southern right whale. Notice the pale growths of rough skin above and below the mouth, called callosities.

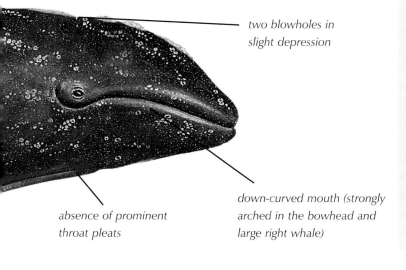

two blowholes in slight depression

absence of prominent throat pleats

down-curved mouth (strongly arched in the bowhead and large right whale)

BOWHEAD WHALE
Bulky body with rounded back. Distinctive white chin. Large down-curved mouth. No callosities. No dorsal fin.

NORTHERN AND SOUTHERN RIGHT WHALES
Head has callosities. Mouth is strongly arched. No dorsal fin.

GREY WHALE
Mottled grey body colour. Slightly down-curved mouth. No callosities. Low hump and knuckles instead of dorsal fin.

PYGMY RIGHT WHALE
Smaller than other right whales. Shaped like a rorqual whale but with down-curved mouth. Dorsal fin is present.

IDENTIFICATION

 Flukes are very wide, with a distinct notch in the middle, and may be raised high in the air on diving. Narrow tail stock. In older whales the flukes may have pale markings.

 Rounded back with no dorsal fin.

 Flippers are black and broad.

 Head is up to one-third of body length, with very large arched jaw. Indentation behind blowhole. Chin is white with 'necklace' of black or grey spots. No callosities.

 Extremely stocky, mostly black body.

 The two blowholes are widely separated and produce a distinctive V-shaped blow up to 7 m (23 ft) high.

 Usually found singly, in pairs or in threes, with larger groups at good feeding grounds.

 Slow swimming. On surfacing, usually visible as two distinct humps – the head and the rounded back. Occasionally breaches, lobtails, flipper-slaps or spyhops. When undisturbed, dives of 4–20 minutes may be followed by 4–6 blows at 15- to 30-second intervals.

Bowhead Whale

Bowhead whales belong to the same taxonomic family as the larger right whales (Balaenidae). Bowheads are whales of arctic and subarctic waters. They penetrate farther north than any other whale, and with their muscular blubber-rich bodies they can break through pack ice to breathe. The bowhead whale is readily recognisable by its white chin and its massive head, which extends to nearly one-third the length of the body. The head houses enormous baleen plates that can reach more than 4 m (13 ft) long – the largest of any whale. The bowhead skim-feeds for krill, copepods and other zooplankton at various levels in the water column. Because of their slow swimming speed and bulky, blubber-rich body, bowheads were, along with other large right whales, favoured species for hunting. By 1900 the bowhead was nearly extinct but has since made a reasonable comeback. The bowhead is named after its skull. With the flesh removed, the skull is narrow and strongly arched, looking like a bow.

Above: Two bowhead whales 'nuzzling' in Isabella Bay, Baffin Island, Nunavut.

FACTFILE

Scientific name: *Balaena mysticetus*
Family: Balaenidae
Range: Arctic and subarctic waters
Habitat: Waters at edge of pack ice
Status: Vulnerable
Population: Fewer than 10,000
Diet: Animal plankton such as krill and copepods
Length: 12–20 m (40–65 ft); females larger than males
Weight: 60–100 tonnes

WHERE TO WATCH

Watching choice: Baffin Island, Nunavut, Canada.
When to go: May to September. Whales follow the melting edge of the sea ice early in the season and then stay to breed.

| ☐ Ocean | ◼ Known range | ☐ Permanent ice |

Getting there: The regional transport hub to Baffin Island is Iqaluit, Nunavut's capital city, which has flight connections to Ottawa and Montreal.

Southern & Northern Right Whales

FACTFILE

Scientific name: *Eubalaena australis* (southern), *Eubalaena glacialis* (North Atlantic), *Eubalaena japonica* (North Pacific)
Family: Balaenidae
Range: Southern Atlantic, Indian and Pacific (southern right); northern Atlantic and Pacific (northern right)
Habitat: Coastal waters especially, but also oceanic
Status: Vulnerable (southern); endangered (northern)
Population: Fewer than 8,000/400 (southern/northern)
Diet: Crustaceans and zooplankton
Length: 11–18 m (36–59 ft); females larger than males
Weight: 50–80 tonnes

IDENTIFICATION

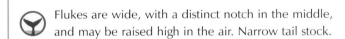 Flukes are wide, with a distinct notch in the middle, and may be raised high in the air. Narrow tail stock.

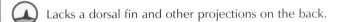 Lacks a dorsal fin and other projections on the back.

 Flippers are broad and black or dark brown.

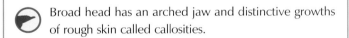 Broad head has an arched jaw and distinctive growths of rough skin called callosities.

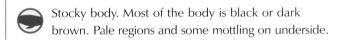 Stocky body. Most of the body is black or dark brown. Pale regions and some mottling on underside.

 Two blowholes. V-shaped blow up to 5 m (16 ft) high.

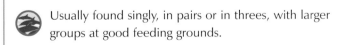 Usually found singly, in pairs or in threes, with larger groups at good feeding grounds.

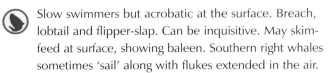 Slow swimmers but acrobatic at the surface. Breach, lobtail and flipper-slap. Can be inquisitive. May skim-feed at surface, showing baleen. Southern right whales sometimes 'sail' along with flukes extended in the air.

The southern and northern right whales are similar in appearance and among the easiest of all whales to identify. They swim slowly, often close to the surface, and pale growths of rough skin on their heads, infested with whale lice and barnacles, are highly distinctive. Like grey whales and humpbacks, right whales migrate along predictable sea highways. Unfortunately, such features have made these whales among the easiest to hunt. They have been heavily exploited since medieval times and, although protected internationally since the 1930s, both species remain vulnerable to extinction. The northern right numbers only a few hundred and, in the face of collisions with ships, entanglement in nets and habitat deterioration, its survival hangs by a thread. Recently, scientists found the northern right whale to be two species: the North Atlantic form, *Eubalaena glacialis*, and the North Pacific form, *Eubalaena japonica*. Surprisingly, the North Pacific right whale is more closely related to the southern right whale, *Eubalaena australis*, than to its North Atlantic relative.

WHERE TO WATCH

Watching choice: Península Valdés, Patagonia, Argentina (southern right whale).
When to go: Mid-July to November; peak season September to October.
Getting there: Day tours go from Puerto Madryn, Puerto Pirámide and Trelew. Longer excursions operate from Buenos Aires, which is the regional transport hub.

☐ Ocean
☐ Permanent ice
◼ North Pacific right whale
◼ North Atlantic right whale
◼ Southern right whale

Left: A southern right whale in Patagonia, Argentina, with its flukes raised to form a 'sail'. Whales sail across bays in this fashion perhaps as a form of play.

Grey Whale

FACTFILE

Scientific name: *Eschrichtius robustus*
Family: Eschrichtiidae
Range: North Pacific Ocean
Habitat: Coastal waters
Status: Locally common
Population: 23,000–25,000
Diet: Bottom-living invertebrates, especially amphipod and isopod crustaceans, and segmented worms
Length: 11–15 m (36–49 ft); females larger than males
Weight: 25–35 tonnes

IDENTIFICATION

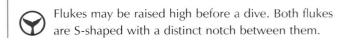 Flukes may be raised high before a dive. Both flukes are S-shaped with a distinct notch between them.

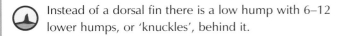 Instead of a dorsal fin there is a low hump with 6–12 lower humps, or 'knuckles', behind it.

 Flippers are broad with pointed tips.

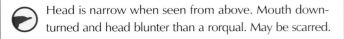 Head is narrow when seen from above. Mouth down-turned and head blunter than a rorqual. May be scarred.

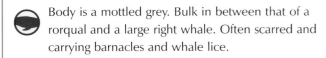 Body is a mottled grey. Bulk in between that of a rorqual and a large right whale. Often scarred and carrying barnacles and whale lice.

 Bushy, heart-shaped or V-shaped blow 4 m (13 ft) high.

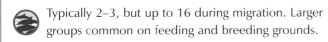 Typically 2–3, but up to 16 during migration. Larger groups common on feeding and breeding grounds.

Slow swimming. Not afraid of boats and sometimes inquisitive. Frequently spyhops. May breach, lobtail or flipper-slap. On feeding grounds, may dive for 15 minutes, sending up clouds of seabed sediment. On migration, when undisturbed, dives of 3–5 minutes followed by 3–6 blows at 15- to 30-second intervals.

One of the most distinctive whales, this blunt-headed, scarred and barnacled baleen whale is a whale watcher's favourite. Its head shape and body bulk are in between that of a large right whale and a rorqual. Like the larger right whales, this slow-swimming, coast-hugging cetacean was heavily hunted for hundreds of years. Since the species was protected in 1946, the eastern Pacific population has made a strong comeback. The western Pacific population remains sparse, with only a few hundred individuals.

The eastern Pacific grey is well-known for its long-distance migrations between summer feeding grounds in the Bering, Beaufort and Chukchi seas of subarctic and arctic waters and winter calving grounds off Baja California, Mexico. For many individuals, the annual round trip is about 18,000 km (11,000 miles). Among baleen whales, the grey whale is uniquely a bottom-feeder. In its northern feeding grounds, it will bury its snout in the sediment, engulfing a mouthful of mud and water, which it strains through the baleen. Most individuals roll onto their right side to feed, and the head is more scarred and the baleen more worn on that side.

WHERE TO WATCH

Watching choice:
The lagoons of Baja California, Mexico.
When to go:
January to April.
Getting there:
Boat- and/or shore-based whale-watching tours operate out of San Diego, La Paz, Ensenada, Rosarito and Tijuana. Major regional transport hubs are San Diego, Tijuana and La Paz.

☐ Ocean   ◼ Known range   ☐ Permanent ice

Left: Grey whale spyhopping off Baja California, Mexico, where they calve between January and February. Notice the scarred skin and barnacles.

Watching Sperm Whales

There are three species of sperm whale: the largest, called simply the sperm whale, and two much smaller species, the pygmy and dwarf sperm whales. The sperm whale is the largest toothed whale, reaching a length and weight comparable to that of medium-sized baleen whales. The sperm whale remains widespread and abundant despite intensive hunting for nearly 300 years. Two substances – spermaceti from the whale's head and ambergris from its gut – were highly prized by whalers. Spermaceti, an oil that solidifies on cooling, helped lubricate the 19th-century Industrial Revolution in Europe and North America. Ambergris, a greasy substance from the congealed beaks of digested squid, was used as a fixative in perfumes.

Below: The spermaceti organ, showing its physical features. So-called 'junk' spermaceti is thicker than ordinary spermaceti.

Above: The eye of a young sperm whale. It can see bioluminescent light produced by deep-sea creatures such as squid, octopuses and fish

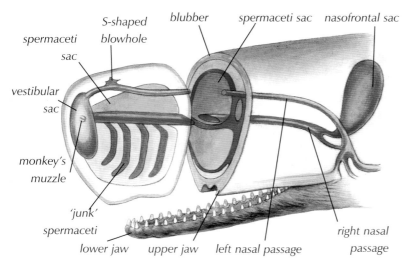

spermaceti sac

vestibular sac

S-shaped blowhole

blubber

spermaceti sac

nasofrontal sac

monkey's muzzle

'junk' spermaceti

lower jaw   upper jaw   left nasal passage

right nasal passage

IDENTIFICATION

The sperm whale, with its huge, squarish head and wrinkly prune-like skin on the rear two-thirds of the body, is relatively easy to recognise. It has a dorsal hump and knuckles instead of a dorsal fin. Its blow is angled forward and to the left at about 45° to the horizontal, so even at long range it can be readily distinguished from other large whales. In comparison to the sperm whale, the pygmy and dwarf species have smaller heads, with blowholes set farther back from the snout. Both have obvious dorsal fins, although that of the dwarf species is larger than the pygmy species.

DIVING

All three species of sperm whale are deep divers that hunt mainly for squid and octopuses. The larger species is legendary in sometimes diving to more than 1,980 m (6,500 ft) in search of giant squid – the world's largest invertebrate at up to 18 m (60 ft) long. These astonishing dives, which can last up to two hours, can take the whale from sunlit tropical surface waters of 25°C (77°F) to lightless, chilly depths of about 2°C (36°F). The spermaceti in the head, when it becomes chilled, probably becomes denser and solidifies, helping the whale sink. When it is time to surface, the whale may divert warm blood to the spermaceti organ, making the spermaceti melt and expand, thus making the whale more buoyant. This buoyancy theory has been recently disputed, and other possible functions for the spermaceti organ include focusing sound beams and acting as a shock absorber for males, which butt each other in disputes over females.

Below: Dwarf sperm whale, showing some physical features characteristic of sperm whale species in general.

SPERM WHALE
Very large blunt head about one-third of body length. Blowhole near the tip of the snout. Dorsal hump.

PYGMY SPERM WHALE
Blunt head about one-sixth of body length. Blowhole slightly forward of the eyes. Small dorsal fin.

DWARF SPERM WHALE
Blunt head about one-sixth of body length. Blowhole above the eyes. Larger dorsal fin.

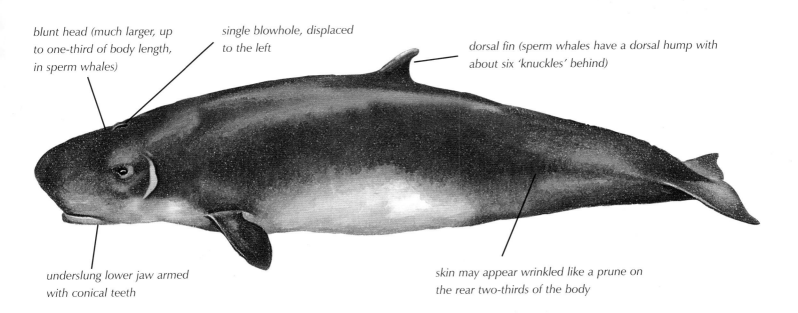

blunt head (much larger, up to one-third of body length, in sperm whales)

single blowhole, displaced to the left

dorsal fin (sperm whales have a dorsal hump with about six 'knuckles' behind)

underslung lower jaw armed with conical teeth

skin may appear wrinkled like a prune on the rear two-thirds of the body

Sperm Whale

The deep-diving ability of sperm whales and the aggressiveness of threatened adult males are legendary. In the early days of whaling, harpooned males rammed and sunk whaling vessels much larger than themselves. Moby Dick, the legendary white whale of Herman Melville's novel, was a sperm whale.

Sperm whales have a highly developed echolocation system to locate their fast-swimming prey in deep water. Their repertoire of sounds includes groans, whistles, and squeaks that are communications with other sperm whales. Some scientists speculate that sperm whales can focus sound beams through the spermaceti organ with sufficient intensity to stun prey.

Sperm whales have a social structure different from that of all other large whales. First, male sperm whales are much larger than females. Second, females and young whales of both sexes tend to stay in temperate or warmer waters all year round, while many adult males remain in cooler waters. The biggest males, traveling singly or in small groups, migrate to warmer waters to compete with each other for females. The heads of males often bear scars from teeth rakes gained during fights with other males.

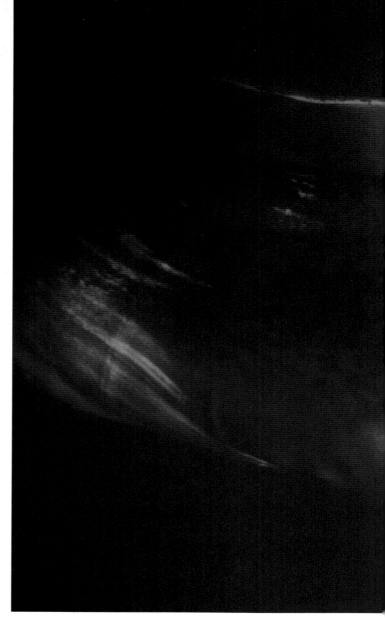

Above: Sperm whales socializing underwater. Notice their large, blunt heads, the short, stubby flippers, and the prune-like skin behind the head.

WHERE TO WATCH

Watching choice: The Azores in the North Atlantic Ocean.
When to go: May to October, when males, females, and calves are present.

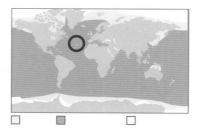

Getting there: Land-based lookout points and boat trips operate from most islands. International flights to Faial, São Miguel, and Terceira. Flights and ferry crossings operate between the islands in the Azores group.

FACTFILE

Scientific name: *Physeter macrocephalus*
Family: Physeteridae
Range: Atlantic, Indian, and Pacific oceans
Habitat: Deep water
Status: Locally common
Population: 300,000–400,000
Diet: Squid, octopuses, and fish
Length: 49–59 ft (15–18 m); females smaller
Weight: Males 38–55 tons; females 20–27 tons

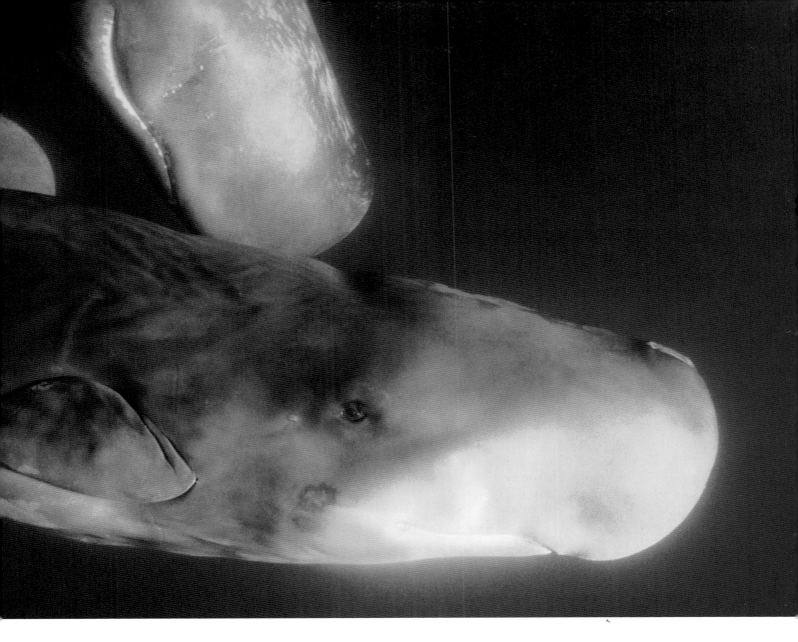

IDENTIFICATION

 Flukes are broad and triangular, with a prominent notch.

 Low hump with about 6 knuckles behind.

 Flippers are fairly short and stubby.

 Blunt head is up to one-third of body length. Underslung toothed lower jaw. Blowhole is near tip of snout and displaced slightly to the left.

 Body colour is dark grey to purplish brown. Last two-thirds of the body is usually wrinkled like a prune.

 Blow is angled forward and to the left at about 45° to the horizontal.

 Females typically in groups of 10–20 animals, including juveniles of both sexes; 'bachelor' males in groups of 10–20; larger males in small groups or travelling alone, except during the breeding season.

 Normally slow swimming but can rapidly accelerate if disturbed. Often lies almost motionless on the surface (logging). Occasionally breaches or lobtails. After a dive of 20–100 minutes, 20–70 blows usually follow at 12- to 20-second intervals.

IDENTIFICATION

 Trailing edge of flukes is S-shaped, with a conspicuous notch in between.

 The dorsal fin of the dwarf sperm whale is like that of a bottlenose dolphin; that of the pygmy sperm whale is similar, but comparatively smaller.

 Flippers are short and broad and located far forward on the body.

 Squarish head with false gill behind each eye. Lower jaw is underslung and quite small.

 Small, stocky body. Back is black, dark grey or blue-grey. Underside is pale blue, grey or pinkish.

 Blowhole is displaced to the left. In pygmy sperm whale, it is located slightly forward of the eyes; in dwarf species, above the eyes. Blow is directed forward but indistinct.

 Usually found singly, in pairs or occasionally in small groups (particularly for the dwarf species).

 Unusual dive sequence, with the whale rising horizontally to the surface and then sinking again. May float almost motionless at surface (logging). May evacuate gut contents if disturbed.

Pygmy & Dwarf Sperm Whales

The pygmy (see illustration below) and dwarf (see p. 60) sperm whales are little-known. It is quite tricky to tell the two species apart and much of the information about them has come from stranded specimens.

Both species have a wide distribution in warmer oceanic waters, with the dwarf sperm preferring the edge of the continental shelf and the pygmy sperm deeper water. At sea, both species could be confused for a bottlenose dolphin but for the blunt head without a beak and the presence of a false gill behind the eye. The dwarf sperm whale has a relatively larger dorsal fin than the pygmy. Both species commonly float almost motionless in the water. When disturbed, they may evacuate the contents of their gut to produce a reddish brown foul-smelling cloud. This probably acts as a distraction or deterrent to potential predators, allowing the small whale to make its escape.

Pygmy and dwarf sperm whales are sufficiently distinct from the sperm whale to be placed in a taxonomic family of their own, the Kogiidae.

Above: A pygmy sperm whale calf stranded in Florida.

FACTFILE

Scientific name: *Kogia breviceps* (pygmy sperm whale); *Kogia simus* (dwarf sperm whale)
Family: Kogiidae
Range: Temperate, subtropical and tropical waters of the Atlantic, Indian and Pacific oceans
Habitat: Oceanic (pygmy); offshore (dwarf)
Status/Population: Unknown for both species
Diet: Squid, octopuses, fish and crustaceans
Length: 2.4–3.4 m (8–11 ft); dwarf slightly smaller
Weight: Pygmy sperm whale 320–400 kg (700–880 lbs); dwarf species slightly smaller

WHERE TO WATCH

Watching choice: Dominica, Caribbean Sea.
When to go: December to June; peak season for seeing all three sperm whale species is March to April.

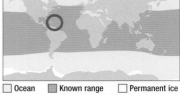

| Ocean | Known range for both species | Permanent ice |

Getting there: International flights to Melville Hall Airport, Dominica. Boat excursions for whale watching depart from Roseau and its surroundings.

Watching Beaked Whales

Whale experts have described about 21 species of beaked whale; all are members of the family Ziphiidae (the ziphiids). Although they are toothed whales, in most species only the adult males have erupted teeth – two or four in the lower jaw – and they probably use their teeth as tusks to fight with other males for access to females. Beaked whales swallow their prey whole and feed largely or entirely on squid, octopuses and soft-bodied fish that inhabit the twilight and lightless depths of the oceans. Most beaked whales spend little time at the surface. Their deep-diving habits, along with the difficulty of identifying them except at close range, mean that beaked whales are among the least studied and understood of all whales.

IDENTIFICATION

Four features help distinguish beaked whales from other cetaceans. First, they have beaks – but these whales are larger than beaked dolphins. Second, unlike most other cetaceans, their flukes lack a notch in the middle. Third, compared to other cetaceans of similar size, the dorsal fin is of moderate size and located about two-thirds back along the body. Finally, adult males usually have two or four prominent teeth. When identifying the species, head features and geographic location are important indicators.

Above: The pale, goose-shaped head of Cuvier's beaked whale surfacing off North Carolina.

Below: Shepherd's beaked whale, showing physical features characteristic of most beaked whale species.

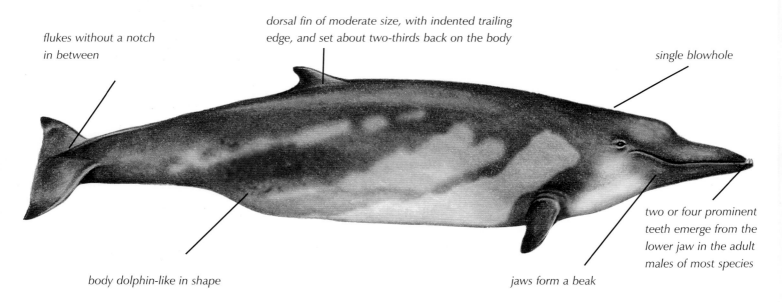

flukes without a notch in between

dorsal fin of moderate size, with indented trailing edge, and set about two-thirds back on the body

single blowhole

two or four prominent teeth emerge from the lower jaw in the adult males of most species

body dolphin-like in shape

jaws form a beak

BEAKED WHALES

BAIRD'S BEAKED WHALE
Darkly pigmented with a slightly bulbous forehead. North Pacific.

ARNOUX'S BEAKED WHALE
Very similar to Baird's beaked whale. Southern Hemisphere.

NORTHERN BOTTLENOSE WHALE
Very bulbous, pale melon and comparatively short, pale beak.

SOUTHERN BOTTLENOSE WHALE
Very similar to northern bottlenose but melon and beak slightly darker.

CUVIER'S BEAKED WHALE
Very short beak, upturned mouth and pale head.

SHEPHERD'S BEAKED WHALE
Narrow beak. Boldly marked in bands of dark brown and cream. Southern Hemisphere.

LONGMAN'S BEAKED WHALE
Strongly domed forehead. Adult males have two small teeth at tip of lower jaw. Tropical waters.

STRAP-TOOTHED (LAYARD'S) WHALE
Adult male has two large backward-curving teeth in middle of lower jaw. Southern Hemisphere.

GRAY'S BEAKED WHALE
Snout long, narrow, and pale. Two teeth in adult male halfway along mouthline. Cool temperate Southern Hemisphere.

HUBBS' BEAKED WHALE
Pale, moderately short beak. Pale domed forehead. Arched jaw in males with two teeth halfway along. North Pacific.

STEJNEGER'S BEAKED WHALE
Similar to Hubbs' but upper beak usually dark. Forehead dark and not obviously domed. North Pacific.

TRUE'S BEAKED WHALE
Adult males have two small teeth at tip of lower jaw. North Atlantic and southern Indian oceans.

SOWERBY'S BEAKED WHALE
Similar to True's but adult males have two teeth halfway along jawline.

BLAINVILLE'S BEAKED WHALE
Strongly arched jaw. Adult males have two teeth at top of arch.

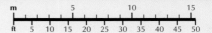

GINGKO-TOOTHED BEAKED WHALE
Named after the adult male's two large teeth, shaped like ginkgo leaves. Tropical to temperate Indian and Pacific oceans.

SPADE-TOOTHED BEAKED WHALE
Species recently determined based on skeletal remains. Males have teeth similar to strap-toothed, but broader. Eastern and western temperate Pacific.

ANDREWS' BEAKED WHALE
Body dark. Beak pale. Lower jaw arched with two exposed teeth in males. Cool temperate waters off Australasia.

GERVAIS' BEAKED WHALE
Narrow beak and slightly bulging forehead. Males have two small teeth in middle of lower jaw. Temperate to tropical Atlantic.

HECTOR'S BEAKED WHALE
Similar to True's whale but upper jaw pale. Temperate Southern Hemisphere.

PERRIN'S BEAKED WHALE
Almost identical in appearance to Hector's beaked whale. North Pacific Ocean off California.

LESSER (PYGMY) BEAKED WHALE
Moderately short, dark-tipped beak. Jaw arched. Eastern and western tropical to temperate Pacific.

Baird's & Arnoux's Beaked Whales

Baird's (see illustration below) and Arnoux's are the largest beaked whales. They are extremely similar in appearance; indeed, some scientists consider them to be the same species. Both have slender beaks, and adults of both sexes have four protruding teeth at the front of the lower jaw, of which only the front two are normally visible when the mouth is closed. The size and position of the teeth, along with the shape of the head, distinguish them from other beaked whales.

Both species are deep divers, descending for up to an hour to hunt. Arnoux's appears to be more social. Pods of six to 10 are quite common, with gatherings of up to 80 individuals on occasion. Group sizes in Baird's seem to be smaller. Arnoux's is one of the few whales that hunts beneath the pack ice in the Southern Ocean.

Above: Baird's beaked whales. Notice the dorsal fin set far back on the body.

WHERE TO WATCH

Watching choice:
Monterey Bay,
California.
When to go:
September to
October.
Getting there:
Offshore whale-
watching excursions leave from Monterey and Santa Cruz in California. The regional transport hub is San Francisco.

| Ocean | Baird's beaked whales |
| Permanent ice | Arnoux's beaked whales |

FACTFILE

Scientific name: *Berardius bairdii* (Baird's beaked whale); *Berardius arnuxii* (Arnoux's beaked whale)
Family: Ziphiidae
Range: Northern Pacific (Baird's); southern Atlantic, Indian and Pacific oceans, and Southern Ocean (Arnoux's)
Habitat: Coastal/oceanic waters near steep, deep slopes
Status/Population: Unknown for both species
Diet: Mid-water and deepwater squid and fish
Length: Baird's 9–12.5 m (30–41 ft); Arnoux's 7.6–9.8 m (25–32 ft). Males slightly smaller than females
Weight: Baird's 11–15 tonnes; Arnoux's 7–10 tonnes

IDENTIFICATION

 Flukes are broad with small, or no, notch in the middle. Trailing edges are slightly concave or almost straight.

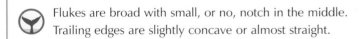 Dorsal fin is small and set two-thirds back along body. Trailing edge usually indented and tip slightly rounded.

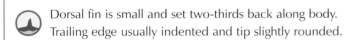 Flippers are fairly short and wide (for a beaked whale) with rounded tips.

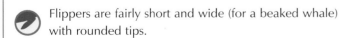 Head has a bulbous melon and a distinct beak. The lower jaw extends beyond the upper, and two teeth are visible at the tip of the lower jaw in both sexes.

 Body colour fairly uniform black, dark grey or brown. Parallel pale scars (probably caused by teeth of mating partners or rivals) in older specimens.

 Blow is low, bushy and indistinct.

 Baird's in groups of 3–10, occasionally up to 30. Arnoux's in groups of 6–10, occasionally up to 80.

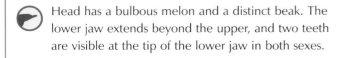 Normally dive in groups that surface at the same time. Dives last 15 minutes to an hour. Beak may surface first. Occasionally lobtail, spyhop or even breach. May lie at surface for about 5 minutes before diving again.

Northern & Southern Bottlenose Whales

FACTFILE

Scientific name: *Hyperoodon ampullatus* (northern); *Hyperoodon planifrons* (southern)
Family: Ziphiidae
Range: Northern Atlantic (northern); southern Atlantic, Indian and Pacific oceans, and Southern Ocean (southern)
Habitat: Deep oceanic waters
Status: Low risk for both species
Population: Unknown for both species
Diet: Squid, fish and bottom-living invertebrates
Length: 6–10 m (19–33 ft)
Weight: 6–8 tonnes

IDENTIFICATION

 Flukes are broad with no, or small, notch in the middle.

 Dorsal fin is set back on body. Trailing, indented edge.

 Flippers are small with convex trailing edges.

 Whitish or pale grey beak and bulbous melon with indentation beneath. Lower jaw extends beyond upper. Two teeth visible at tip of lower jaw in adult males.

 Body colour from dark grey to brown (northern) or tan to grey-brown (southern). Creamy brown or pale grey underside (both). Young whales are darker than adults.

 Blow projects slightly forward about 1.9 m (6 ft) high.

 Groups of 4–10, but up to 35 (northern). Groups of 2–10, occasionally up to 25 (southern).

 Dives last 10–60 minutes. Occasionally lobtail or breach. May lie at surface for 10 minutes or more, blowing every 30–40 seconds, before diving again.

The northern (see illustration below) and southern bottlenose whales are two species separated from each other by thousands of miles. They live in cool temperate waters in different hemispheres. Although similar in appearance, and seemingly in behaviour, their histories of exploitation are very different. Norwegian, British and Canadian whalers intensively hunted the northern species between the 1850s and mid-1900s, and their numbers may remain depleted. The southern bottlenose was rarely if ever hunted and probably remains the most common beaked whale in southern polar and subpolar waters.

With their bulbous forehead and light-coloured melon and beak, adult bottlenoses are readily distinguishable from other beaked whales at close range. Their name comes from the shape of their beak, which is compared to an old-fashioned round-bottomed bottle. Bottlenose whales dive deep to feed on squid and fish, but also take bottom-living animals such as starfish and sea cucumbers. Both species will feed close to pack ice and, like Arnoux's whales, they deep-dive in near freezing conditions.

WHERE TO WATCH

Watching choice: Cruise ships to Antarctica for the southern bottlenose whale.
When to go: Late November to March.
Getting there: Cruise ships leave from various ports in Australia, New Zealand and South Africa, but especially Argentina and Chile in South America. Cruises typically of 21 days or more.

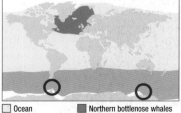

☐ Ocean   ■ Northern bottlenose whales
☐ Permanent ice   ■ Southern bottlenose whales

Left: A northern bottlenose whale with her calf. Notice the broad, slightly concave flukes and the dorsal fin set far back on the body.

IDENTIFICATION

 Flukes are broad with no, or a small, notch in the middle. Trailing edges are slightly concave.

 Dorsal fin is set well behind the centre of the body. Trailing edge is usually indented, but occasionally straight, and the tip is slightly rounded.

 Flippers are small. Convex trailing edges and rounded tips.

 Short, slightly upturned beak. Mostly cream coloured in front of eyes, and behind the head in old males. Two teeth usually visible at tip of lower jaw in adult males.

 Body colour varies from rusty brown to dark grey. Underside often slightly darker. Adults may appear mottled because of circular or oval scars from cookie-cutter sharks or lampreys.

 Blow is low, bushy and indistinct.

 Typically in groups of 2–7, occasionally up to 25. Older males tend to be more solitary.

 Sometimes curious. Dives typically last between 20 and 40 minutes. Occasionally projects head at a shallow angle above the surface or breaches near vertical. Usually arches back steeply when diving.

Cuvier's Beaked Whale

Cuvier's beaked whale is widely distributed from tropical to temperate waters and is fairly common. Whale watchers sometimes liken its pale head, with its short, slightly upturned beak, to that of a goose. Adult males have two small teeth protruding from the front of the lower jaw and their pale coloration often extends to the shoulders.

Until recently, Cuvier's beaked whale was best known from stranded specimens. At sea, close-up views are needed to distinguish this species from other beaked whales, in particular the bottlenose whales of cooler waters and the little-known Longman's beaked whale of warmer waters. Immature and female Cuvier's have duller coloration than adult males and so are easier to confuse with other species. As with other small- to medium-sized beaked whales, Cuvier's has escaped the intensive hunting inflicted on many larger whale species. Like other beaked whale species, Cuvier's is a deep diver. It prefers deep-sea squid and fish but will hunt bottom-living fish and invertebrates as well.

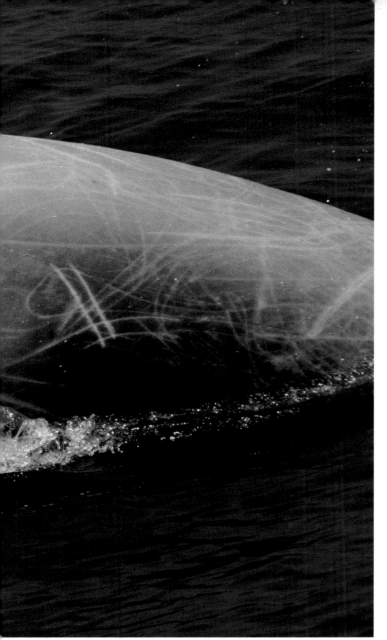

Above: A Cuvier's beaked whale surfacing off North Carolina.

FACTFILE

Scientific name: *Ziphius cavirostris*
Family: Ziphiidae
Range: Widespread in Atlantic, Indian and Pacific oceans
Habitat: Oceanic and coastal waters close to steep gradients such as underwater canyons
Status/Population: Unknown
Diet: Mid-water or deepwater squid, fish and crustaceans
Length: 5.5–7 m (18–23 ft)
Weight: 2–3 tonnes

WHERE TO WATCH

Watching choice: Bay of Biscay between France and Spain, North Atlantic Ocean.
When to go: March to May, when Cuvier's beaked whales are concentrated there.

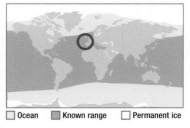

☐ Ocean ☐ Known range ☐ Permanent ice

Getting there: Ferry-based whale-watching excursions to the Bay of Biscay operate from Portsmouth, England, and Bilbao, Spain.

True's Beaked Whale

FACTFILE

Scientific name: *Mesoplodon mirus*
Family: Ziphiidae
Range: North Atlantic and southern Indian oceans in warm temperate and subtropical waters
Habitat: Oceanic waters close to continental slopes
Status/Population: Unknown
Diet: Mid-water or deepwater squid
Length: 4.9–5.5 m (16–18 ft); females larger than males
Weight: 1–1.3 tonnes

IDENTIFICATION

 Flukes are broad and typically without a notch in the middle. Trailing edges are slightly concave.

 Dorsal fin is set about two-thirds back on the body. Trailing edge is indented and tip slightly rounded.

 Flippers are fairly narrow with nearly pointed tips and slightly convex trailing edges. Coloration is usually similar above and below.

 Slightly domed melon and medium-sized beak. Jaw is paler below than above. Has a dark patch around each eye. Adult males have two slightly protruding teeth at the tip of lower the jaw.

 Streamlined body tends to be dark blue or brownish grey above and slightly paler below. In the southern form, a wide pale region may extend from the vent area to dorsal fin and back to just before tail stock.

 Blow is low and indistinct.

 The few sightings have been of 1–3 individuals.

 Seen emerging from a dive with the head at a steep angle. Occasionally breaches. Seems to dive without raising its flukes.

True's beaked whale is named after museum curator Frederick W. True, who in 1913 described a specimen stranded in North Carolina. He gave this *Mesoplodon* species the tag *mirus*, meaning 'wonderful'. In 2001 an adult whale breached 24 times alongside a ferry in the Bay of Biscay and it was photographed at sea for the first time. The rare image opposite was captured that day.

There appear to be two populations of True's whales, one in the North Atlantic and one in the southern Indian Ocean. There are differences in body pigmentation and skull structure in specimens from the two populations and they may well represent subspecies. The specimen depicted opposite is a North Atlantic male.

In the localities where they occur, True's beaked whales could be confused with Cuvier's, Blainville's or Sowerby's beaked whales. Cuvier's has a short beak, whereas in Blainville's the beak is strongly arched. True's beaked adult males have two small teeth visible at the tip of the lower jaw, whereas in Sowerby's they are in the middle. The southern form of True's beaked whale is extremely similar to Hector's beaked whale and Longman's beaked whale, which occur in the same locality.

WHERE TO WATCH

Watching choice: Bay of Biscay between France and Spain, North Atlantic Ocean.
When to go: March to July.

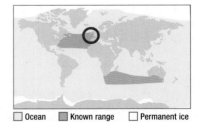

☐ Ocean ■ Known range ☐ Permanent ice

Getting there: Ferry-based whale-watching excursions to the Bay of Biscay operate from Portsmouth, England, and Bilbao, Spain.

Left: A rare photograph of a True's beaked whale at sea. This male is breaching in the Bay of Biscay. Note the visible eye patches.

Sowerby's Beaked Whale

FACTFILE

Scientific name: *Mesoplodon bidens*
Family: Ziphiidae
Range: North Atlantic Ocean; adjacent subarctic waters
Habitat: Oceanic and coastal waters above or close to deep water
Status/Population: Unknown
Diet: Mid-water or deepwater squid and fish
Length: 4–5.5 m (13–18 ft); males larger than females
Weight: 1–1.3 tonnes

IDENTIFICATION

 Flukes are broad and without a notch. Trailing edges are slightly concave. Dark coloration above and below.

 Dorsal fin is set well back behind the centre of the body. Trailing edge is indented and tip slightly rounded.

 Flippers are moderately large for a beaked whale, with nearly pointed tips and convex trailing edges. Darker on upper surface than below.

 Head is narrow for a beaked whale, with a moderately long beak and distinct bulge in front of the blowhole. Mouth line is straight. Two teeth (one on each side) are usually visible in middle of lower jaw in adult males.

 Streamlined body is a drab grey with a slightly paler underside. Scars from cookie-cutter sharks may give a slightly mottled appearance.

 Blow is low, bushy and indistinct.

 Usually single or in pairs. Occasionally in mixed-sex groups of up to 8–10 individuals, including calves.

 Typically dives for 10–15 minutes, but sometimes up to 30 minutes. Occasionally seen emerging from a dive with the head at a steep angle.

Left: A rare image of Sowerby's beaked whale. The prominent beak, the bulge in front of the blowhole and the dorsal fin set far back are evident.

Sowerby's beaked whale is also called the North Atlantic beaked whale and, like the northern bottlenose whale, its distribution is restricted to that locality. Sowerby's was the first beaked whale to be named. English watercolour artist James Sowerby identified it in 1804 from a specimen stranded in Moray Firth, Scotland. However, little is known about the live animal. It is relatively unobtrusive and rarely displays at the surface, although sometimes after a dive its head emerges from the water at a steep angle.

Sowerby's beaked whale has a fairly slim beak and a narrow head with a bulge just in front of the blowhole. Sowerby's can be mistaken for Blainville's, Gervais' or True's beaked whales, all of which are *Mesoplodon* species that can be found in the same locality. Adult Sowerby's males have two teeth (one on each side) about halfway along the lower jaw. In adult True's males the teeth are at the tip of the jaw, and in adult Blainville's males they are on a raised platform in the middle of the jaw. Gervais', the species that is most similar to Sowerby's, has smaller teeth located slightly farther forward. Females or juveniles of all four species may be impossible to reliably distinguish at sea.

WHERE TO WATCH

Watching choice: The Azores in the North Atlantic Ocean.
When to go: May to October.
Getting there: Boat excursions operate from

Ocean   Known range   Permanent ice

most islands, but especially Faial, Flores, Pico and São Miguel. International flights to Faial, São Miguel and Terceira. Flights and ferry crossings operate between the islands in the Azores group.

IDENTIFICATION

 Flukes are broad and typically without a notch. Trailing edges slightly concave. Colour dark above, pale below.

 Dorsal fin is set about two-thirds back on body. Trailing edge indented or almost straight. Tip slightly rounded.

 Flippers are small with nearly pointed tips and slightly convex trailing edges. Colour variable above and below.

 Head is narrow for a beaked whale. Flattened forehead and moderately long beak. Mouthline highly distinctive, with abrupt arching about halfway along lower jaw. In adult males two teeth (one on each side) usually visible in middle of lower jaw. Barnacle growths common, making them appear dark.

 Streamlined body is a dark bluish grey or brown above with a paler underside. Scattered pale or tan blotches.

 Blow is low and projects forward but is indistinct.

 Usually single, in pairs or in small groups of up to 6 individuals, but occasionally up to 12.

 Typically dives last 20–30 minutes. Occasionally emerges from dive with head at a steep angle.

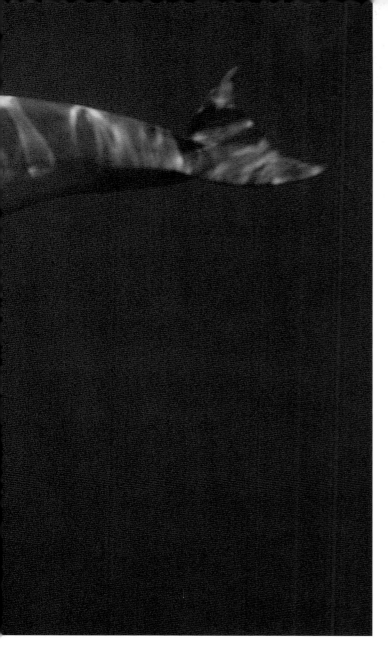

Blainville's Beaked Whale

Blainville's beaked whale was described in 1817 from a remarkable fragment of jawbone. On testing, the bone was found to be even denser than elephant ivory, giving the whale its other common name, the dense-beaked whale. Various theories have been proposed as to why this whale has the densest bone in the animal kingdom. Scientists currently favour the theory that it provides protection for males when they head butt each other in fights over females.

Blainville's beaked whale is widely distributed between temperate and tropical waters. Quite similar in appearance to Sowerby's beaked whale, its most striking difference is the highly arched lower jaw. In adult males, two teeth emerge from the top of the arch like tusks. In some individuals, barnacles grow on the teeth and give the appearance of two pompons stuck on top of the whale's head.

Blainville's is one of the few beaked whales with wild populations that have been closely studied for long periods.

Above: A female Blainville's beaked whale swimming in Hawaiian waters.

FACTFILE

Scientific name: *Mesoplodon densirostris*
Family: Ziphiidae
Range: Temperate to tropical waters in the Atlantic, Indian and Pacific oceans
Habitat: Oceanic waters above continental slopes, especially those close to deep gulleys
Status/Population: Unknown
Diet: Mid-water or deepwater squid and fish
Length: 4–5.8 m (13–19 ft); males larger than females
Weight: About 1 tonne

WHERE TO WATCH

Watching choice: Bahamas, in the Caribbean Sea.
When to go: January to August.
Getting there: 10-day wildlife conservation

Ocean ☐ Known range ■ Permanent ice ☐

expeditions operating from Sandy Point, Great Abaco Island, Bahamas, can be booked through European operators. You can work alongside scientists to study the beaked whales and dolphins in the locality.

Watching White Whales

Except for the bowhead whale, the narwhal and beluga are the only cetaceans that live in arctic or subarctic waters all year round. The narwhal and beluga have many similarities, including overall shape and size. They are the only two living members of the family Monodontidae, from the Greek for 'single-toothed'. This name is inaccurate, since the beluga has 32–36 teeth and the narwhal has two in the upper jaw. The narwhal's teeth do not normally erupt except in adult males, where one tooth grows forward from the left side of the upper jaw as a tusk. The narwhal and beluga are more commonly called 'white whales': adult belugas are uniformly pale, whereas adult narwhals are heavily mottled but become paler in old age.

IDENTIFICATION

The narwhal and beluga are relatively small whales and are easy to identify because of their distinctive features and restricted geographic range. They both have bulbous heads, little or no beak and broad flippers, and both lack a dorsal fin. Their flukes are convex with a distinct notch in the middle. The beluga, being entirely white or pale yellow, is unmistakable as an adult. Adult narwhals are mottled black or brown against a pale body, and males have a highly distinctive tusk.

Below: The narwhal, showing physical features characteristic of the beluga as well.

WHERE TO LOOK

Although narwhals and belugas live in the same geographic region, they are only occasionally found in close proximity. Both species are deep divers and can plunge to 1,000 m (3,300 ft) or more to consume creatures on, or close to, the sea bottom. Belugas enter shallow estuaries in summer, often gathering in the hundreds or thousands to feed on migrating salmon and other fish. In winter, many beluga populations migrate away from the advancing pack ice to reach ice-free

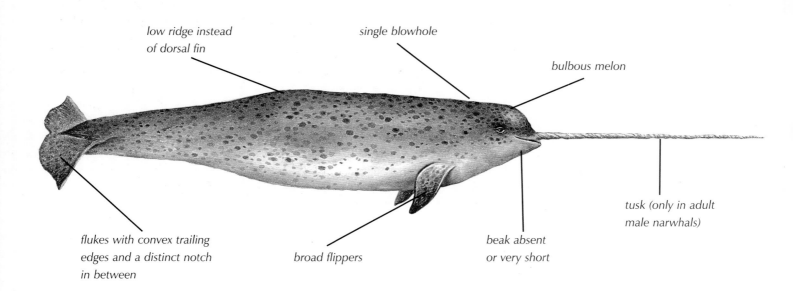

low ridge instead
of dorsal fin

single blowhole

bulbous melon

flukes with convex trailing
edges and a distinct notch
in between

broad flippers

beak absent
or very short

tusk (only in adult
male narwhals)

waters. Belugas seem better able than narwhals to manoeuvre in shallow water. Belugas can even successfully refloat themselves after being stranded for several hours, providing a polar bear has not found them first.

Narwhals have a slightly more northerly distribution. They are at home among pack ice and commonly gather in gaps in ice floes where they might avoid the attention of killer whales. In summer, they enter deep bays and fjords to feed. As winter approaches, narwhals migrate southward in large aggregations of hundreds or even thousands. In the depths of winter, narwhals scatter, often remaining in small pods of the same sex and age. Large aggregations also form in spring as the ice retreats and the narwhals migrate northward. Within these aggregations, large males, young males and females with juveniles often remain in separate groups.

IN CAPTIVITY

Along with killer whales and bottlenose dolphins, belugas are among the cetaceans most commonly put on display in sealife parks and oceanariums. With their striking pale coloration and wide range of facial expressions, belugas are a popular attraction. The tide of popular opinion is gradually shifting against keeping wild cetaceans in captivity.

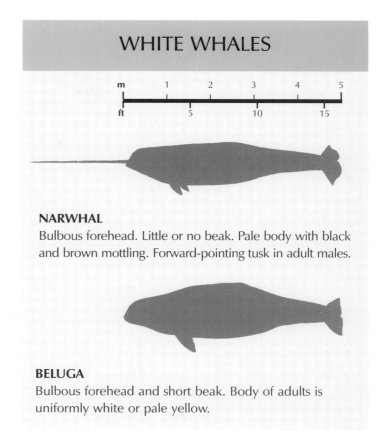

WHITE WHALES

NARWHAL
Bulbous forehead. Little or no beak. Pale body with black and brown mottling. Forward-pointing tusk in adult males.

BELUGA
Bulbous forehead and short beak. Body of adults is uniformly white or pale yellow.

Below: Narwhals congregate in a break in an ice floe. Here they are relatively safe from killer whales, but may be vulnerable to attacks from polar bears.

Narwhal

FACTFILE

Scientific name: *Monodon monoceros*
Family: Monodontidae
Range: Arctic and subarctic waters
Habitat: Coastal waters, including among pack ice
Status: Unknown
Population: 40,000–60,000
Diet: Fish, squid and shrimp
Length: 3.3–5.2 m (11–17 ft)
Weight: 0.8–1.6 tonnes

IDENTIFICATION

 Flukes have strongly convex trailing edges and a deep notch in the middle.

 Dorsal fin is absent. Low ridge instead.

 Flippers are dark grey, short and usually curled up at the tips.

 Head has a bulbous melon and a very short beak. Adult males have a long, forward-pointing tusk.

 Body colour ranges from uniform grey in calves to purplish black in juveniles to black or brown mottling on a pale grey or white background in adults.

 Blow is indistinct. In quiet conditions, it is more likely to be heard than seen.

 Usually in groups of 2–10, but up to hundreds in dispersed herds when travelling.

 Often dives in groups that surface more or less at the same time. Dives usually last 7–20 minutes. Occasionally lobtails, spyhops or flipper-slaps. May rest at the surface for 5–10 minutes before diving again.

Adult male narwhals, with their unique spiral tusk, are the stuff of myths and legends. As late as the 17th century, traders had a vested interest in claiming that the tusks came from unicorns, and they were sold as such, fetching high prices. Some male narwhals grow two tusks, and occasionally a female grows one. Scientists have long argued over the function of the tusk, with ideas ranging from its use as a probe to disturb creatures on the sea bottom, to a device to drill through ice, to a spear to impale prey. Almost certainly the tusk is a display of health and vigour, and males use it in ritualised combat over access to females. In spring, adult males can sometimes be seen clashing their tusks above the water surface.

A narwhal changes colour as it grows older. As a newborn it is almost uniformly grey and at one to two years old it turns purplish black. As the animal grows into adulthood, small black or brown blotches predominate, with a pale background gradually spreading upward from the underside. In old age, the blotches become fewer and the pale colour dominates.

Indigenous peoples in Greenland and northern Canada continue to take several hundred narwhals each year for a wide variety of whale products.

WHERE TO WATCH

Watching choice: Nunavut, Canada.
When to go: June to August. Whales follow the melting edge of the sea ice.

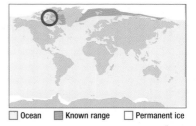

☐ Ocean ▪ Known range ☐ Permanent ice

Getting there: Boat trips leave from Baffin Island. The regional transport hub is Iqaluit, Nunavut's capital city, which has flight connections to Ottawa and Montreal.

Left: Three male narwhals 'sparring' with their tusks, which can grow to nearly 3 m (10 ft) long but average about 1.8 m (6 ft).

Beluga

FACTFILE

Scientific name: *Delphinapterus leucas*
Family: Monodontidae
Range: Arctic and subarctic waters
Habitat: Coastal waters, including estuaries and rivers, and close to pack ice
Status: Vulnerable
Population: More than 100,000
Diet: Fish, squid, octopuses, bottom-living crustaceans, molluscs and worms
Length: 3.3–5.5 m (10–18 ft); females smaller than males
Weight: 0.7–1.6 tonnes

IDENTIFICATION

 Flukes have convex trailing edges, sometimes tinged dark brown, and a deep notch in the middle.

 Dorsal fin is absent. Low ridge instead.

 Flippers are short and sometimes curled up at the tips, especially in older males.

 Head has a bulbous melon and a very short beak.

 Body colour gradually changes from uniform grey in calves to completely white or pale yellow in adults.

 Blow is indistinct. In quiet conditions, it is more likely to be heard than seen.

 Usually in groups of 5–15, but up to hundreds or thousands in and around river estuaries in summer.

 Slow swimmer. Sometimes curious. Commonly lobtails or spyhops. Deep dives usually last 1–10 minutes, interspersed with several breaths at the surface.

Early whalers dubbed the beluga the 'sea canary' because of its wide repertoire of sounds. These include squeaks, clicks, twitters, creaking sounds and moos, which can even be heard through the hull of a boat. Apart from their stunning pure white or pale yellow colour, belugas are also unusual among cetaceans in having very mobile, expressive mouths and flexible necks. Whether changes in facial expression simply accompany other actions, such as sucking in prey or making sounds, or have meanings in themselves is unknown.

Like narwhals, belugas change colour as they grow, but unlike narwhals, belugas are never blotchy. Slate grey when born, belugas gradually whiten until they are five to 10 years old. Young belugas can be confused with young narwhals, but both tend to be found among adults of their own species, aiding identification.

In total, several thousand belugas are killed every year by indigenous peoples in Alaska, Canada, Greenland and Russia, but chemical pollution is also a threat. Belugas in the St Lawrence River, for example, contain high concentrations of contaminants that, when combined, make these animals more liable to congenital deformities and cancers.

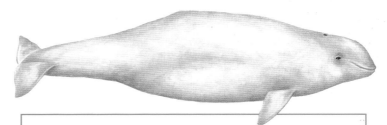

WHERE TO WATCH

Watching choice: Churchill River estuary, Manitoba, Canada.
When to go: July to September. More than 3,000 belugas feed on schooling fish in the vicinity.
Getting there: Daily flights from Winnipeg, Manitoba, to Churchill.

☐ Ocean ▨ Known range ☐ Permanent ice

Left: A beluga spyhopping near Somerset Island, Nunavut, where belugas are watchable in July and August.

Watching Blackfish

These six species of whales – rather misleadingly dubbed 'blackfish' by early whalers because of their dark coloration – are actually members of the dolphin family (Delphinidae). Four species of blackfish – the killer whale, the two pilot whale species and the false killer whale – are much larger than other members of the dolphin family. The two remaining blackfish species – the melon-headed whale and the pygmy killer whale – are of similar size to many oceanic dolphins. Among the blackfish, killer whales, false killers and pygmy killers hunt other marine mammals in the wild, but do not behave with direct aggression toward people. Blackfish live in social groups and sometimes swim with other cetacean species.

IDENTIFICATION

With their dark coloration, blunt heads and prominent dorsal fins, blackfish – especially the larger species – are comparatively easy to distinguish from other small whales or large dolphins. The killer whale, with its bold black-and-white markings and its upright dorsal fin, is one of the easiest cetaceans to identify. The remaining blackfish species can be distinguished from one another by their overall size; the contours of their heads; and the shape, size and position of their dorsal fins and flippers.

Above: A short-finned pilot whale swimming off Tenerife, Canary Islands. The large, low, backward-curved dorsal fin is an identifying feature.

Below: The short-finned pilot whale, showing physical features characteristic of other blackfish.

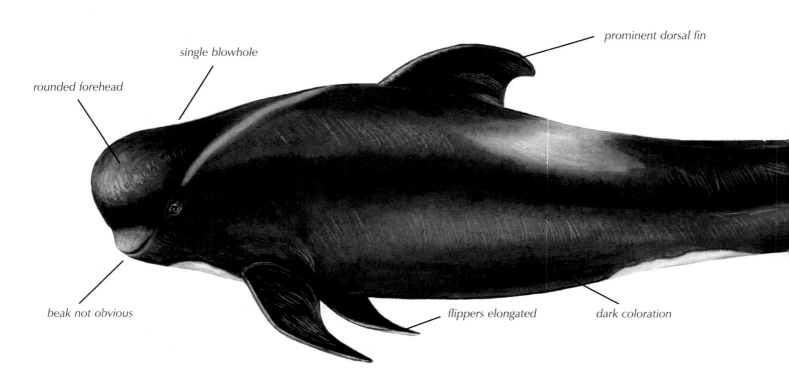

single blowhole

rounded forehead

prominent dorsal fin

beak not obvious

flippers elongated

dark coloration

MELON-HEADED WHALE

Named after its characteristically pointed head, which lacks a beak, the melon-headed whale, *Peponocephala electra*, was originally thought to be a dolphin species. It was only in the 1960s that dead specimens were studied in enough detail to reveal their closer affinity with blackfish rather than to other groups within the dolphin family. The melon-headed whale reaches a maximum size of about 160 kg (355 lbs) – that of a medium-sized dolphin – and feeds on fish and squid.

Like the pygmy killer, the melon-headed whale lives in tropical and subtropical waters, and prefers deep oceanic water. In some parts of the world it will approach boats and even bow-ride. The melon-headed whale is difficult to distinguish from the pygmy killer whale or juvenile false killer whales, except at close range. However, the melon-headed whale often gathers in large groups of 100 to 500 individuals, and if seen in such large numbers, the animal is likely to be a melon-headed whale rather than a pygmy killer whale.

PYGMY KILLER WHALE

The pygmy killer whale, *Feresa attenuata*, like the melon-headed whale, is the size of a dolphin rather than a whale. The biggest specimens weigh only about 170 kg (375 lbs). The pygmy killer is surprisingly aggressive for its size. In captivity, and in the wild, it has been observed attacking other cetaceans of similar size. Pygmy killers commonly swim in groups of 10 to 30 animals, often in line abreast, but are rarely seen on whale-watching trips. They usually hunt squid and fish but will take small marine mammals such as seals.

flukes have a distinct notch

BLACKFISH

KILLER WHALE

The largest blackfish. Distinctive black-and-white coloration. Tall, triangular dorsal fin in males; smaller and more curved in females.

SHORT-FINNED PILOT WHALE

Very similar to the long-finned pilot whale, but flippers slightly shorter and tends to live in warmer waters.

LONG-FINNED PILOT WHALE

Bulbous forehead. Upturned mouth. Low, broad, backward-curved dorsal fin set forward of the midline. Very long, slender flippers positioned close to the head.

FALSE KILLER WHALE

Rounded head. Straight mouth. Flippers shorter than in a pilot whale.

MELON-HEADED WHALE

Head more pointed than in the false killer whale. Mouth usually with white, pale grey or pink 'lips'. Flippers have fairly pointed tips.

PYGMY KILLER WHALE

Head more rounded than in the melon-headed whale. Mouth with white 'lips'. Flippers have rounded tips.

Killer Whale

FACTFILE

Scientific name: *Orcinus orca*
Family: Delphinidae
Range: All oceans, with cooler waters preferred
Habitat: Coastal and oceanic waters
Status: Locally common
Population: Well in excess of 100,000
Diet: Varied, from fish and squid to marine mammals
Length: 6–9.8 m (20–32 ft); males larger than females
Weight: 3–9 tonnes

IDENTIFICATION

 Flukes have slightly concave trailing edges and a distinct notch. Upper side is dark and underside pale.

 Tall dorsal fin is slightly forward of midline. Triangular in adult males and curved in adult females.

 Flippers are black or dark grey. Broad with rounded tips.

 Head has slightly rounded melon and gently tapered snout. Upper head is black with a bold white patch behind each eye. Chin and throat are white.

 Black upper body with grey 'saddle' just behind the dorsal fin. Bold white curved patch extends into each flank from the white underside.

 Blow is low and bushy. Visible in cool, still air.

 Usually in family or social groups (pods) of 3–25. Several pods may gather temporarily.

 Often inquisitive and playful. May breach, lobtail, flipper-slap and spyhop. Sometimes rolls to slap dorsal fin on surface. When travelling, a common dive pattern is 4–5 dives of less than 30 seconds each, followed by a longer dive of 5–10 minutes.

The killer whale, the subject of several Hollywood movies and numerous television documentaries since the 1970s, is one of the best known of all whales. Scientists have been studying the killer whale populations off the Pacific coast of North America for more than 40 years. The killer whale, so named by early whalers because of its attacks on other whales, is a supremely accomplished hunter. It fine-tunes its hunting strategy according to the prey available locally. Described as 'the wolves of the sea', killer whales cooperate within social groups to overpower prey larger than themselves. Despite their sinister name, killer whales in the wild are not known to attack people. Indeed, they are now recognised as animals of some considerable intelligence and great social cohesion.

In some parts of the world scientists have described three kinds of killer whales. Resident (local) killer whales form social groups (pods), typically of 10 individuals or more, which roam within a predictable range year after year. Transient (traveller) killer whales travel in smaller pods, roam more widely in shallow water and seem to specialise in hunting warm-blooded prey – other marine mammals and occasionally birds. Offshore killer whales live in deeper water, travel in larger pods, tend to be smaller in size and hunt mostly fish. Scientists can tell the three forms apart, not just by their habits but also by their physical characteristics, such as subtle differences in the shape and size of their dorsal fins and in their grey saddle patches.

WHERE TO WATCH

Watching choice: Tysfjord, Norway.
When to go: October to early December, when herring and the killer whales that feed on them are concentrated in the fjord.

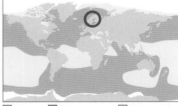

☐ Ocean   ■ Known range   ☐ Permanent ice

Getting there: Regional transport hubs for road and rail are Narvik and Fauske; Evenes and Bodø are the nearest airports. All have daily bus connections to Tysfjord.

Left: A killer whale spyhopping in Tysfjord, Norway. The local killer whale population is observable on boat safaris between October and January.

CHANGING ATTITUDES

In the 1950s, killer whales were commonly regarded as a danger to humans and major competitors for depleting fish stocks. However, it is now known that humans, through overfishing, are more responsible than orcas for the depletion of fish stocks, and there is no reliable evidence of killer whales attacking humans. Orca watching is now a thriving industry that supports, and is supported by, ongoing scientific research.

PODS

A typical killer whale family group consists of two to nine individuals: an elderly mother and two or more generations of her descendants and their close relatives. Family units often gather in larger social groups ranging from 60 to more than 100 individuals. The family groups and the larger groups are generically called 'pods'.

HUNTING STRATEGIES

Killer whales show a diversity of hunting strategies. A herring-hunting pod in Alaska, for example, will swim around a school of fish, scaring them into a tight ball

Above: Killer whale attacking a grey whale calf off Monterey Bay, California. Several killers will separate a grey whale mother from her calf before attacking.

just beneath the sea surface. One or more members of the pod then swim through the bait ball, slapping the water with their flukes to produce shock waves that stun the fish. The dazed fish can then be eaten.

In the Southern Ocean, killer whales cooperate by nudging ice floes to disturb seals or penguins resting on them. Other whales wait on the floe's opposite side to snatch animals as they enter the water. In Patagonia, Argentina, killer whales have learned how to swim through the surf and beach themselves to grab sea lion pups from the beach before wriggling to get back into the water. They teach this remarkable strategy to their young.

Right: Five killer whales off the San Juan Islands, Washington State. The shape and size of the dorsal fins suggest they are females and/or young males.

tall, triangular dorsal fin (curved in females)

slightly rounded melon and gently tapered snout

grey 'saddle'

flukes with slightly concave trailing edges

broad flippers with rounded tips

bold black-and-white coloration

Long- & Short-Finned Pilot Whales

FACTFILE

Scientific name: *Globicephala melas* (long-finned);
Globicephala macrorhynchus (short-finned)
Family: Delphinidae
Range: Temperate–subpolar regions of all oceans except
North Pacific (long-finned); tropical to warm temperate
Atlantic, Indian and Pacific oceans (short-finned)
Habitat: Offshore and oceanic
Status: Both species common
Population: In excess of 500,000/185,000 (long/short)
Diet: Mostly squid and schooling fish
Length: 4–7.6 m (13–25 ft); short-finned larger
Weight: 1.8–3.5 tonnes; short-finned heavier

IDENTIFICATION

 Flukes have concave trailing edges and a distinct notch.

 Dorsal fin is low, long and broad-based, with a rounded tip and trailing edge that is usually strongly concave.

 Flippers are long, narrow and swept back. About one-fifth of body length in long-finned species.

 Bulbous melon and short beak. Sometimes a pale stripe extends diagonally upward from each eye.

 Body is largely dark grey, black or brown. May be a grey saddle patch behind the dorsal fin. White or pale grey patch on belly and W-shaped area on the throat.

 Strong blow up to 1.2 m (4 ft) high.

 Groups of 10–60, but up to hundreds or thousands.

 Commonly lobtails or spyhops, and sometimes logs. Shallow dives last 2–6 minutes, deep dives 10 minutes or more. Dives are interspersed with several breaths.

Pilot whales are recognisable by their blunt heads, dark bodies and broad, curved-back dorsal fins. The two species (long-finned, below; short-finned, p. 86) are difficult to tell apart at sea because their flippers – the key distinguishing feature – are not readily visible unless they breach or spyhop. However, the two species favour different water temperatures – the short-finned species preferring warmer – and their distributions overlap only slightly. The long-finned species has two distinct populations, one in the Northern Hemisphere and the other in the Southern.

Pilot whales usually travel in groups of 10 to 60, and sometimes come together in thousands. Long-finned pilots are the most commonly stranded whale, and when one individual strands, others in the pod stay with it and usually strand as well. More than 1,000 long-finned pilot whales are killed each year for whale products by Faeroe islanders. Japanese whalers continue to take several hundred short-finned pilot whales annually.

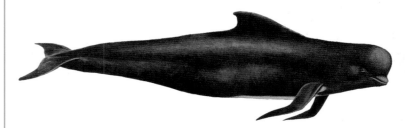

WHERE TO WATCH

Watching choice: La Gomera, Canary Islands (for the short-finned pilot whale).
When to go: March to November. More than 500 pilot whales frequent the waters between La Gomera and Tenerife.
Getting there: Whale-watching excursions go from La Gomera. Flight connections go to La Gomera and Tenerife.

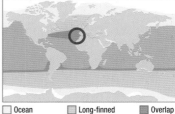

☐ Ocean	☐ Long-finned	☐ Overlap
☐ Permanent ice	☐ Short-finned	area

Left: The head and shoulders of a short-finned pilot whale, seen from above. The blunt head, single blowhole and broad-based dorsal fin are evident.

False Killer Whale

FACTFILE

Scientific name: *Pseudorca crassidens*
Family: Delphinidae
Range: Tropical to mild temperate regions of the Atlantic, Indian and Pacific oceans
Habitat: Offshore and oceanic
Status: Unknown
Population: In excess of 50,000
Diet: Varied, from fish and squid to marine mammals
Length: 3.7–6 m (12–19.5 ft)
Weight: 1.1–2.2 tonnes

IDENTIFICATION

 Flukes have concave trailing edges and a distinct notch in the middle.

 Fairly prominent dorsal fin in the centre of the back, with a strongly concave trailing edge.

 Flippers are long, narrow and swept back, with a distinctive bulge on the leading edge.

 Head is darker than the body, with a rounded snout and a straight mouthline.

 The body is almost entirely dark grey or black. A W-shaped region on the throat is white or pale grey.

 Blow is indistinct.

 Usually in groups of 10–50, but up to hundreds on occasion. Sometimes accompanied by bottlenose dolphins.

 A fast-swimming, acrobatic whale. It commonly approaches boats and bow-rides or wake-rides. May arc gracefully through the air. Commonly breaches, falling back into the water on its side with a large splash.

This sleek predator is much smaller than the killer whale and lacks its bold black and white markings. It is of similar length to long- and short-finned pilot whales, but is more streamlined and has a more dolphin-like appearance. Its behaviour is also dolphin-like, as it leaps entirely out of the water and rides the bow waves of passing vessels. The false killer is about twice the length of the pygmy killer and melon-headed whales, with which it might otherwise be confused.

False killer whales, like their larger namesakes, have a varied diet and can hunt a wide range of prey. Like killer whales, they fine-tune their hunting strategy according to the prey species locally available. Observers have reported them attacking and eating dolphins and even taking bites out of sperm whales. They have a reputation for stealing high-value fish, such as tuna, caught on baited longlines set by fishermen.

Like the long-finned pilot, the false killer seems to be particularly susceptible to stranding, and schools of several hundred sometimes run aground. In June 2005, about 100 false killers beached in Geographe Bay, Western Australia, and were refloated by more than 1,000 volunteers working under the guidance of experts.

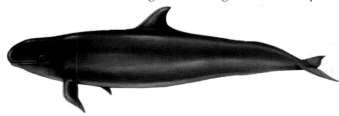

WHERE TO WATCH

Watching choice: Hawaii (big island).
When to go: All year-round.
Getting there: Keahole (Kona) Airport on the big island (Hawaii) can

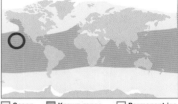

☐ Ocean ■ Known range ☐ Permanent ice

be reached directly or by short flight from Honolulu Airport on the nearby island of Oahu. Suitable boat excursions leave the big island from Honokohau, Kailua-Kona, Keauhou and Kohala Coast.

Left: An unusual view of a false killer whale mother and calf. Notice the dark head, grey body and distinctive bulge on the leading edge of the flippers.

Watching Oceanic Dolphins without Prominent Beaks

The 14 species of cetacean included here are all oceanic dolphins (family Delphinidae) that lack a prominent beak. Short-beaked dolphins belong to three different subfamilies: Cephalorhynchinae, Delphininae and Orcaellinae. Other members of the Delphinidae have distinct beaks. Many of the short-beaked oceanic dolphins look superficially like porpoises (see pp. 136–143). However, they have conical teeth rather than the spade-shaped teeth of porpoises and are less secretive.

IDENTIFICATION

This group is highly variable in shape, size and colour, save for the absence of a prominent beak. As in other dolphins and in most porpoises, the flukes are notched in the middle and the dorsal fin is quite prominent and usually positioned about halfway back on the body. Chilean (black), Heaviside's, Hector's and Commerson's

Above: Four Hector's dolphins. Their dark, rounded dorsal fins, blunt snouts and bold markings, in grey, white and black, are clearly visible.

Below: An Atlantic white-sided dolphin, showing physical features characteristic of most dolphins that lack a prominent beak.

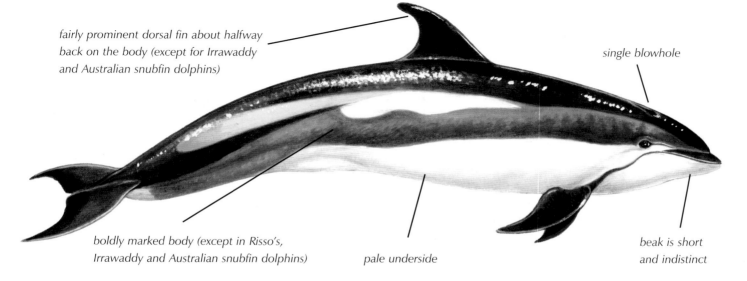

fairly prominent dorsal fin about halfway back on the body (except for Irrawaddy and Australian snubfin dolphins)

single blowhole

boldly marked body (except in Risso's, Irrawaddy and Australian snubfin dolphins)

pale underside

beak is short and indistinct

OCEANIC DOLPHINS WITHOUT PROMINENT BEAKS

RISSO'S DOLPHIN
Large dolphin with a blunt head and high dorsal fin. Warm seas in Atlantic, Indian and Pacific oceans.

WHITE-BEAKED DOLPHIN
Large, sturdy body with a large dorsal fin. White stripe and two pale grey patches on each flank. North Atlantic.

IRRAWADDY DOLPHIN
Melon-shaped head. Stubby dorsal fin. Rivers and coastal waters of the Indo-Pacific, from India to Australia.

AUSTRALIAN SNUBFIN DOLPHIN
Almost identical to the Irrawaddy dolphin. Identified in 2005. Australia and Papua New Guinea.

FRASER'S DOLPHIN
Stocky body with a black or dark grey stripe along each flank. Warm seas in Atlantic, Indian and Pacific oceans.

ATLANTIC WHITE-SIDED DOLPHIN
Distinctive yellow patch on either side of a very thick tail stock. Cool temperate and subarctic waters of North Atlantic.

PACIFIC WHITE-SIDED DOLPHIN
Pale stripe along each flank and pale grey on trailing edge of dorsal fin. Temperate waters of the North Pacific.

PEALE'S DOLPHIN
Very similar to Pacific white-sided dolphin but with a dark dorsal fin and dark face. Local to Argentina and Chile.

DUSKY DOLPHIN
Pale stripes/patches on each flank. Pale grey trailing edge on dorsal fin. Coastal temperate waters of Southern Hemisphere.

HOURGLASS DOLPHIN
White-on-black hourglass pattern on flanks. Dark dorsal fin. Cool waters of Southern Hemisphere.

CHILEAN (BLACK) DOLPHIN
Mostly black. Pale underside. Rounded dorsal fin. Chilean coastal waters.

HEAVISIDE'S DOLPHIN
Grey-and-black body. Triangular dorsal fin. Coastal southwestern Africa.

HECTOR'S DOLPHIN
Grey-and-black back and flanks. Pale underside. Rounded dorsal fin. Coastal waters of New Zealand.

COMMERSON'S DOLPHIN
Bold black-and-white coloration. Rounded dorsal fin. Coastal South America and offshore islands.

dolphins belong to the subfamily Cephalorhynchinae, and their rounded or triangular dorsal fins distinguish them from other short-beaked dolphins.

SURFACE BEHAVIOUR

Short-beaked dolphins tend to be much more acrobatic than porpoises, often leaping clear of the water. Some species, such as dusky dolphins, even somersault.

When swimming slowly and breaking the surface only slightly, short-beaked dolphins can easily be mistaken for porpoises.

A dolphin's arc-shaped leaps may be an attempt to locate seabirds that are feeding on fish. Falling back into the water with a splash, followed by a lobtail, often accompanies feeding. The activity may scare fish into a tight ball and/or signal to other dolphins the location of fish. Some dolphins somersault, and twist and turn as they breach, usually after a good feeding session.

Risso's Dolphin

FACTFILE

Scientific name: *Grampus griseus*
Family: Delphinidae
Range: Cool temperate to tropical waters of the Atlantic, Indian and Pacific oceans
Habitat: Continental slope and offshore waters, and around oceanic islands
Status: Unknown, but locally common
Population: Unknown
Diet: Squid, octopuses and cuttlefish
Length: 2.6–3.8 m (8½–12½ ft)
Weight: 300–500 kg (660–1,100 lbs)

IDENTIFICATION

 Flukes have concave trailing edges and a notch in the middle. The tail stock is narrow when viewed from above.

 Dorsal fin is tall with a concave trailing edge.

 Flippers are long and tapered, similar to those of pilot whales.

 Blunt head has a bulbous melon. Mouth is curved upward. Chin is pale.

 Upper body is grey or brown, often with extensive scarring. Underside is pale.

 Usually in groups of 3–30, but 'superpods' of several thousand are occasionally reported.

 May be playful and acrobatic and leap, spyhop, flipper-slap or lobtail. When travelling, typically dives for 1–2 minutes interspersed by 6–12 breaths at 15- to 20-second intervals. Feeding dives can last up to 30 minutes. Sometimes swims in mixed schools with other cetaceans such as bottlenose dolphins or pilot whales.

Left: A Risso's dolphin breaching near the Maldives in the Indian Ocean. The blunt head, tall dorsal fin and long flippers are a distinctive combination.

Risso's dolphin is the largest dolphin. With a bulging forehead, a very upright, curved dorsal fin and a rather battered appearance, its features make it quite distinct from any other species of similar size. The scars scattered over its body are caused by the teeth rakes of other individuals and squid bites. Its body colour is quite variable, from grey through to light brown, with a white underside. Some Risso's dolphins become paler as they age and a few even approach the white or yellow coloration of beluga whales.

Risso's dolphins are widely distributed in warm waters and seem to prefer the water just beyond the continental shelf, where the seabed begins to fall away to depths beyond 300 m (1,000 ft). There they hunt for squid that rise toward the surface at night.

In the wild and in captivity, Risso's dolphins interbreed occasionally with bottlenose dolphins, producing hybrids that have a combination of the features of both species. Risso's dolphin, although little studied, appears to be widespread and common. However, in Japan, Indonesia and some Caribbean and Pacific islands, it is hunted for food.

WHERE TO WATCH

Watching choice: The Azores in the North Atlantic Ocean.
When to go: April to September.
Getting there: Boat excursions operate

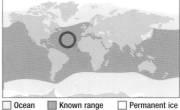

□ Ocean ■ Known range □ Permanent ice

from most islands, but especially Faial and Pico. International flights to Faial, São Miguel, and Terceira; flights and ferry crossings operate between the islands in the Azores group.

IDENTIFICATION

 Flukes have concave trailing edges and a notch in the middle. Dark above and below.

 Large black dorsal fin with a curved trailing edge.

 Flippers are black. Moderately large with pointed tips.

 Has a short beak that is usually white, but may be grey or even black. A white throat and grey forehead.

 The upper back is black around the dorsal fin and grey toward the head and tail. A white blaze runs back along each flank leading to two grey patches in the rear half. The underside is mostly white.

 Usually in groups of 5–50, with up to several hundred on occasion. Sometimes assemble alongside feeding fin whales, humpback whales or killer whales, or in mixed schools with other dolphin species.

 May bow-ride or wake-ride. Is sometimes playful and acrobatic. May porpoise, leap high, breach or lobtail. When swimming fast, it may raise its whole body slightly out of the water to breathe, leaving a curtain of spray, called a 'rooster tail', behind it.

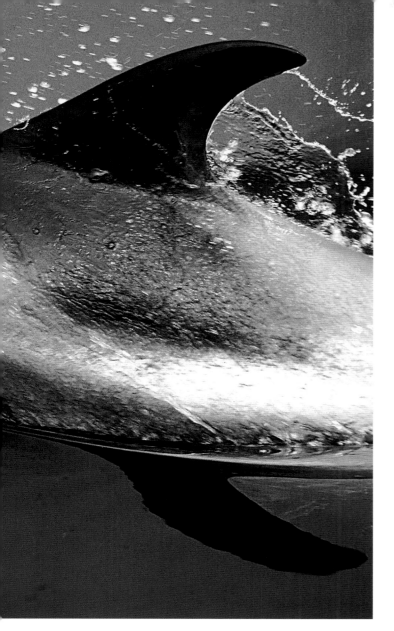

Above: A close-up of a white-beaked dolphin, showing its pale markings.

White-Beaked Dolphin

This robust dolphin with a short, thick beak has a name that accurately applies only to some members of the species. Many European white-beaked dolphins do have pale beaks, but those living in North American waters, on the western side of the Atlantic Ocean, may have beaks that are grey or black.

The white-beaked dolphin has the most northerly distribution of any dolphin, and some schools enter icy subarctic waters in summer. In most of its range, the white-beaked dolphin could be confused with the Atlantic white-sided dolphin, which is of similar shape and size. However, the white-sided species has an upper back that is uniformly dark from head to tail, whereas the white-beaked dolphin has pale grey regions near the head and tail.

The white-beaked dolphin prefers the shallow waters of the continental shelf and feeds on fish and invertebrates at all levels in the water column, from the surface to the seabed.

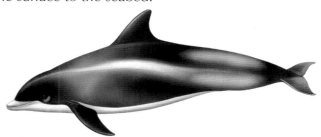

FACTFILE

Scientific name: *Lagenorhynchus albirostris*
Family: Delphinidae
Range: Cool temperate and subarctic North Atlantic
Habitat: Shallow coastal and estuarine waters
Status: Unknown, but locally common
Population: Unknown
Diet: Small fish, squid and crustaceans
Length: 2.6–3.2 m (8½–10½ ft); males slightly larger than females
Weight: 180–275 kg (400–600 lbs)

WHERE TO WATCH

Watching choice:
Iceland, North Atlantic.
When to go: April to September. Baleen whales and harbour porpoises are also watchable here at this time.

☐ Ocean   ■ Known range   ☐ Permanent ice

Getting there: Boat trips leave from Húsavik, Keflavik, Olafsvik, Reykjavik and other ports. The island's transport hub is Reykjavik.

Atlantic White-Sided Dolphin

Like the white-beaked dolphin, this robust dolphin has a short, thick beak and lives in the North Atlantic. It is slightly smaller and less stocky than the white-beaked dolphin, has a slightly less prominent dorsal fin and never has a completely pale beak. Its upper back is entirely black or dark grey, and it has a yellow or tan patch on each flank near the tail stock. This is a similar colour, but in a different position, to that of a common dolphin. Its bold markings make the Atlantic white-sided dolphin one of the most distinctive of all dolphins.

Although the geographic distributions of the Atlantic white-sided and white-beaked dolphins greatly overlap, the white-sided species is found far offshore, in deeper water, as well as inshore in shallow water. It has a varied diet that includes fish and squid as well as bottom-living invertebrates. As with the white-beaked dolphin, individuals in a school may cooperate to herd a school of fish into a tight ball before consuming them.

Above: Leaping Atlantic white-sided dolphins, showing their bold markings.

WHERE TO WATCH

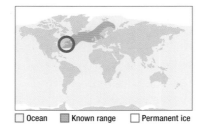

Watching choice: Massachusetts.

When to go: April to October, with various baleen whales watchable at different times.

□ Ocean ■ Known range □ Permanent ice

Getting there: Boat trips leave from Barnstaple, Gloucester, Nantucket, Newburyport, Plymouth and Provincetown. Boston is the regional transport hub.

FACTFILE

Scientific name: *Lagenorhynchus acutus*
Family: Delphinidae
Range: Cool temperate North Atlantic
Habitat: Coastal and offshore waters
Status: Unknown, but locally common
Population: Unknown
Diet: Small fish, squid and crustaceans
Length: 1.9–2.6 m (6½–8½ ft); males slightly larger than females
Weight: 165–230 kg (365–510 lbs)

IDENTIFICATION

 Flukes have concave trailing edges and a notch in the middle. Dark above and below.

 Moderately large black dorsal fin has a curved trailing edge.

 Flippers are black with pointed tips.

 The head has a short beak that is grey or black above and white or pale grey below. The throat is white and the forehead is dark grey or black. There is a dark ring around each eye.

 The upper back is almost uniformly black or dark grey with a white patch and a yellow or tan patch just below. The middle of each flank is grey and the lower part and underside are predominantly white.

 Usually in groups of 5–15, with up to several hundred on occasion. Sometimes assemble alongside feeding fin whales, humpback whales or killer whales, or in mixed schools with other dolphin species.

 May bow-ride or wake-ride. Sometimes playful and acrobatic. May porpoise, leap high, breach or lobtail. When travelling, usually surfaces to breathe every 10–15 seconds.

IDENTIFICATION

 Flukes have concave trailing edges and a notch in the middle. Dark above and below.

 Dorsal fin is dark grey or black on the leading edge and pale grey on the curved trailing edge.

 Flippers are dark and moderately large with pointed tips. In Pacific species the rear two-thirds are pale grey.

 The head has a very short, dark beak. The throat is white, the lower forehead grey, and the upper forehead dark. Has a dark patch around the eyes.

 The upper back is black or dark grey. One or two pale blazes on the dark rear half of the flanks. A large pale patch extends from behind the middle of the head toward the white underside.

 Pacific white-sided in groups of 10–100; dusky in groups of 2–50. Both may gather in groups of more than 1,000. Sometimes assemble alongside feeding baleen whales.

 May bow- or wake-ride, porpoise, leap high, breach or lobtail. When swimming fast, the Pacific white-sided may raise its body out of the water to breathe, leaving a 'rooster tail' spray. Dusky dolphins may twist and turn when diving and sometimes somersault when leaping.

Pacific White-Sided & Dusky Dolphins

The Pacific white-sided (see left illustration below) and the dusky dolphin (see right illustration below) are similar in appearance, but live thousands of miles apart. Both are highly social, often forming large schools that split into smaller groups for feeding and reassemble later. They are highly acrobatic, and their splashes are commonly seen before the animals themselves.

Dusky dolphins are widespread in the Southern Hemisphere and may comprise several populations that rarely interbreed. They prefer shallow coastal waters and take a wide variety of prey between surface waters and the seabed. Pacific white-sided dolphins live offshore in deep North Pacific waters and feed largely on squid and small fish that gather at different levels in the water.

Above: A Pacific white-sided dolphin leaping clear of the water.

FACTFILE

Scientific name: *Lagenorhynchus obliquidens* (Pacific white-sided); *Lagenorhynchus obscurus* (dusky)
Family: Delphinidae
Range: Northern Pacific (white-sided); cooler waters of southern Atlantic, Indian and Pacific oceans (dusky)
Habitat: Offshore and oceanic; coastal waters (dusky)
Status: Both species locally common
Population: Unknown for both species
Diet: Mostly schooling fish and squid
Length: 1.7–2.4 m (5½–8 ft); dusky smaller
Weight: 80–180 kg (175–400 lbs); dusky lighter

WHERE TO WATCH

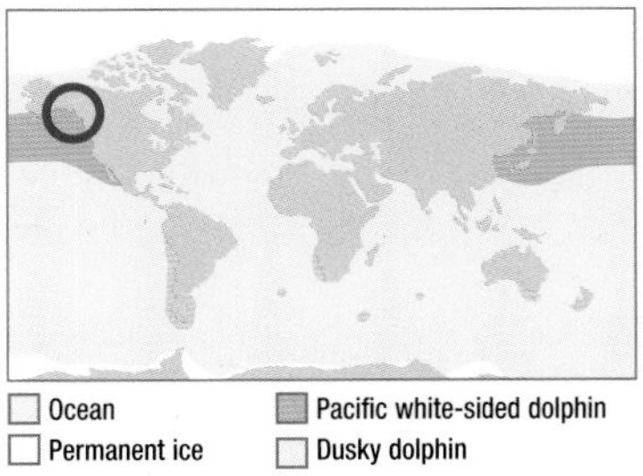

Watching choice: Vancouver Island, British Columbia for the Pacific white-sided dolphin.
When to go: May to September.
Getting there: Boat trips from Port Hardy, Port McNeill, Telegraph Cove and other ports on northern Vancouver Island. Vancouver is the regional transport hub.

☐ Ocean	■ Pacific white-sided dolphin
☐ Permanent ice	☐ Dusky dolphin

Hector's Dolphin

FACTFILE

Scientific name: *Cephalorhynchus hectori*
Family: Delphinidae
Range: New Zealand coastal waters
Habitat: Shallow coastal and estuarine waters
Status: Endangered
Population: Fewer than 5,000
Diet: Small fish, squid and bottom-living invertebrates
Length: 1.2–1.5 m (4–5 ft); females slightly larger than males
Weight: 35–60 kg (75–125 lbs)

IDENTIFICATION

 Flukes have concave trailing edges and a slight notch in the middle. Dark above and below.

 Very distinctive dark, rounded dorsal fin in the middle of the back.

 Flippers are black or dark grey and have rounded tips.

 The blunt head has a black, non-protruding beak. The throat is white and the forehead is grey. A dark band extends from the mouth and eye region to the flipper.

 The upper body is mainly light grey. The underside is white with a dark border. A white region extends into the lower flank and points toward the tail.

 Usually in groups of 2–8, with up to 50 on occasion.

 May bow-ride or wake-ride slow-moving vessels. Sometimes playful and acrobatic. May leap high, breach, or swim upside down. Rarely dives for more than 90 seconds.

This delightful small dolphin, with its blunt head and stocky body, could be mistaken for a porpoise. However, its bold black, white and grey body coloration and rounded dorsal fin distinguish it from any other species of dolphin, or porpoise, in the coastal waters of New Zealand where it lives. Hector's dolphin can be playful and sometimes bow-rides or wake-rides. In winter, the dolphin population moves slightly farther offshore and scatters to find food.

This very local dolphin has been studied in the field since the 1980s, and its high rate of mortality in gill nets set for fish has prompted it to be classified as endangered. Although a sanctuary was created in 1989, where gillnetting is not allowed, elsewhere the animal remains in danger from netting, boat collisions, local pollution and habitat loss through coastal developments such as marinas and fish farms.

There are probably fewer than 5,000 individuals overall, and a subspecies found along the North Island's west coast may number fewer than 100.

WHERE TO WATCH

Watching choice: Banks Peninsula, South Island, New Zealand.
When to go: October to May, when other dolphins are also viewable inshore.

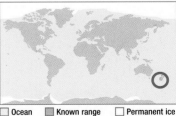

☐ Ocean   ■ Known range   ☐ Permanent ice

Getting there: Boat trips leave from Akaroa Harbour, South Island. International flights go to Christchurch, South Island.

Left: A Hector's dolphin swimming upside down. Its bold black, white and grey coloration is highly distinctive.

Commerson's Dolphin

FACTFILE

Scientific name: *Cephalorhynchus commersonii*
Family: Delphinidae
Range: Coastal waters of Chile, Argentina and the Falkland Islands, and the Kerguélen Islands in the Indian Ocean
Habitat: Coastal waters above the continental shelf
Status: Locally common
Population: Unknown
Diet: Shrimp, small fish, squid and invertebrates
Length: 1.2–1.5 m (4–5 ft); Kerguélen larger than South American
Weight: 35–65 kg (75–145 lbs); Kerguélen heavier than South American

IDENTIFICATION

 Flukes have concave trailing edges and a slight notch in the middle. Dark above and below.

 Distinctive dark, rounded dorsal fin in the middle of the back.

 Flippers are black or dark grey with rounded tips.

 The blunt head has a black, non-protruding beak. The head is boldly black with a white throat patch. In the Kerguélen population, the colour contrasts are less bold.

 A large white patch encircles the body from just behind the head to just forward of the dorsal fin and then extends down each flank. In the Kerguélen population, the colour contrasts are less bold.

 Usually found in groups of 2–3, with up to 100 individuals on occasion.

 May bow-ride or wake-ride fast-moving vessels and ride on breaking waves. May make steep- or low-angle leaps into the air. Commonly swim upside down and rotate as they swim.

Left: Two Commerson's dolphins swimming near the Falkland Islands, South Atlantic Ocean.

Commerson's dolphin is named after the French physician and botanist Philibert Commerson, who first described them in South America's Strait of Magellan in 1767. Being small and stocky with blunt heads, they are sometimes mistaken for porpoises, especially the spectacled porpoise. However, Commerson's black-and-white markings and dorsal fin shape are distinctive, as are its typically dolphin-like surface acrobatics. Around the vent, females have a heart-shaped black patch that points forward. In males, the patch is typically raindrop-shaped and points backward.

There appear to be two distinct populations of Commerson's, one off the coast of Chile, Argentina and the Falkland Islands, and the other about 8,000 km (5,000 miles) to the east around the Kerguélen Islands in the Indian Ocean. Indian Ocean animals are slightly larger than the South American and tend to be marked dark grey on light grey rather than black on white.

Commerson's dolphins appear to be opportunistic feeders, taking prey according to its availability and feeding close to the seabed in shallow water. They are sometimes drowned in gill nets, and South American fishers have been known to dice up captured animals for crab bait, although the practice is now banned.

WHERE TO WATCH

Watching choice: Santa Cruz Province, Patagonia, Argentina.
When to go: December to March, when Peale's dolphin is also viewable.

☐ Ocean   ▪ Known range   ☐ Permanent ice

Getting there: Day tours leave from Puerto Deseado and Puerto San Julián. Buenos Aires is the regional transport hub.

Watching Oceanic Dolphins with Prominent Beaks

The 15 species of cetacean included here are all oceanic dolphins (family Delphinidae) with prominent beaks. The distinctive beak is easy to identify at sea but it is not a taxonomic feature, as dolphins with prominent beaks belong to three different subfamilies (Stenininae, Delphininae and Lissodelphinae), and some members of the Delphininae have indistinct beaks. Dolphins with prominent beaks include five species – the pantropical spotted, Atlantic spotted, spinner, striped and clymene dolphins – that are extremely abundant in warm waters and between them number in the millions. Bottlenose dolphins are probably the best-known cetaceans of all, being a highly visible inhabitant of many coastal regions.

IDENTIFICATION

This group of dolphins is highly variable in shape, size and colour, but most species have a prominent beak with a crease between the beak and forehead. As in other dolphins and in most porpoises, the flukes are notched in the middle and the dorsal fin is quite prominent and usually positioned about halfway back along the body. The northern and southern rightwhale dolphins are unique among dolphins in lacking a dorsal fin.

Above: A group of bottlenose dolphins surfing in waves off South Africa.

Below: A striped dolphin, showing the physical features characteristic of most dolphins that have a prominent beak.

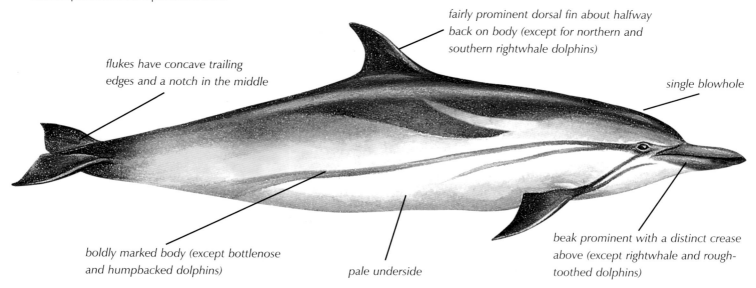

fairly prominent dorsal fin about halfway back on body (except for northern and southern rightwhale dolphins)

single blowhole

flukes have concave trailing edges and a notch in the middle

beak prominent with a distinct crease above (except rightwhale and rough-toothed dolphins)

boldly marked body (except bottlenose and humpbacked dolphins)

pale underside

OCEANIC DOLPHINS WITH PROMINENT BEAKS

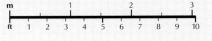

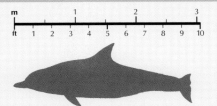

BOTTLENOSE DOLPHIN

Common and Indo-Pacific species. Dark grey on back grades to pale grey on underside. Temperate to tropical waters.

STRIPED DOLPHIN

Distinctive dark stripe along lower flank distinguishes it from other dolphins. Widespread between tropical and warm temperate waters.

NORTHERN RIGHTWHALE DOLPHIN

Very distinctive. No dorsal fin. Black on back and most of flanks. White underside. North Pacific.

INDO-PACIFIC HUMPBACKED DOLPHIN

Distinctive hump on back with a small dorsal fin on top. Indo-Pacific region.

COMMON DOLPHIN

Long- and short-beaked species. Yellow and grey 'hourglass pattern' on flanks. Tropical to warm temperate waters.

SPINNER (LONG-SNOUTED SPINNER) DOLPHIN

Long beak and prominent dorsal fin. Spins as it leaps. Widespread in tropical and subtropical waters.

ATLANTIC HUMPBACKED DOLPHIN

Similar to Indo-Pacific species, but smaller. Tropical west African waters.

SPOTTED DOLPHIN

Pantropical and Atlantic species. Young are unspotted. Tropical to warm temperate waters.

CLYMENE (SHORT-SNOUTED SPINNER) DOLPHIN

A dark cape and short beak. Tropical and subtropical Atlantic.

ROUGH-TOOTHED DOLPHIN

Distinctive, with conical head and a beak that lacks a crease above. Widespread between tropical and warm temperate waters.

SOUTHERN RIGHTWHALE DOLPHIN

No dorsal fin. Similar to northern species, but with white coloration on underside extending to head, flippers and middle of flanks. Southern Hemisphere.

TUCUXI

Similar to a small bottlenose dolphin. Triangular dorsal fin. Rivers and coastal areas of eastern Central America and northeast South America.

SURFACE BEHAVIOUR

When a dolphin leaps high to travel swiftly, called porpoising, it makes three to six rapid fluke beats underwater and then launches itself into the air up to three body-lengths high and three body-lengths forward. As it reenters the water, it creates hardly a ripple. Such leaping is highly energy-efficient.

Leaps that end in side- or belly-slaps are usually forms of communication with other dolphins, with the slap being both a visual and an auditory signal. Acrobatic leaps that include spins and somersaults may be displays of exuberance, but they also serve social roles, enhancing bonding between individuals of the same or opposite sex. Sometimes dolphins leap high to be able to plunge in a steep dive to reach fish they are hunting below.

Bottlenose Dolphin

FACTFILE

Scientific name: *Tursiops truncatus* (common);
Tursiops aduncus (Indo-Pacific)
Family: Delphinidae
Range: Atlantic, Indian and Pacific oceans (common);
Indian and western Pacific oceans (Indo-Pacific)
Habitat: Coastal to oceanic
Status: Common
Population: In excess of 1 million
Diet: Squid, fish and crustaceans
Length: 2–3.8 m (6½–12½ ft)
Weight: 150–650 kg (330–1,430 lbs)

IDENTIFICATION

 Flukes have a notch in the middle, swept-back leading edges, and fairly straight trailing edges that are curved at the ends. Grey above and below.

 Dorsal fin is grey, convex on the leading edge and strongly concave on the trailing edge.

 Grey flippers with curved leading edges and fairly pointed tips.

 Beak is usually grey on the upper side and paler on the lower. Forehead is grey.

 Dark grey cape extends from the shoulders to beyond the dorsal fin, with a lighter grey area across the middle flank and a paler region along the lower flank and underside.

 Inshore common bottlenoses are found in groups of 2–15 individuals. Offshore groups commonly average 20, with up to several hundred on occasion.

 Both species commonly bow-ride, wake-ride, breach and lobtail. Inshore animals rarely dive for more than 3–4 minutes, but offshore animals may do so.

The bottlenose dolphin is the largest of the prominently beaked dolphins and is the species many people bring to mind when they think of a dolphin. It is common in both coastal and offshore waters in many parts of the world, from cool temperate to tropical waters. Compared to most other dolphins, its coloration is quite subdued, grading from dark grey along the back to pale grey or almost white on the underside. In some parts of the world, such as the North Atlantic, two different types (called ecotypes) have been recognised: an inshore form and a slightly larger offshore form that is darker in colour and has slightly smaller flippers. To add to the confusion, since the late 1990s it has been established that there are two species of bottlenose dolphin: the slightly larger and widely distributed common bottlenose dolphin (*Tursiops truncatus*), shown in the illustration below, and the Indo-Pacific bottlenose dolphin (*Tursiops aduncus*), which is restricted to the Indian and western Pacific oceans. The two species are very similar, with Indo-Pacific bottlenoses being slightly smaller and paler than the common species in the same locality. Adult Indo-Pacific bottlenoses usually have spots on their undersides, while the common form rarely does.

WHERE TO WATCH

Watching choice: Monkey Mia, Shark Bay, Western Australia.
When to go: April to October.
Getting there: A managed interaction takes place morning and evening from the shore. Sailboats venture into the bay to see some of the most well-researched wild dolphins in the world. Perth is the regional transport hub.

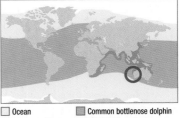

☐ Ocean
☐ Permanent ice
■ Common bottlenose dolphin
■ Indo-Pacific and common bottlenose dolphin

Left: Two captive common bottlenose dolphins leaping in Caribbean waters.

SOCIETY

The social organisation of common bottlenose dolphin groups is complex, and varies between inshore and offshore dolphins and, to some extent, from place to place. In the Gulf of Mexico and along the Florida coast, inshore groups assemble according to age and sex. There are adult male groups, adult female groups with their calves, and immature male groups. Adult male and female groups frequently intermingle, but immature male groups stay separate. The closest social bonds are between males in all-male friendship groups and between mothers, sisters and aunts, and their young offspring, in all-female groups. Groups of adults may join forces for hunting or travelling and, occasionally, for mating. When they do so, status and intent are decided by a complex interplay of postures, gestures, touches and sounds produced by the individuals involved.

Below: A common bottlenose dolphin approaching the camera with an open beak. This could be aggressive behaviour or a form of play.

AGGRESSION

In contrast to their popular image as the gentle dolphin, bottlenose dolphins sometimes act aggressively among themselves and toward other cetaceans. They may chase, bite, ram, tail-slap, blow bubbles, produce a stream of clicks or other sounds and jaw-snap (open and close the jaws rapidly and loudly).

Adult males can gang together to separate a female from her group to mate with her. Males fight with one another to establish a hierarchy, perhaps determining who has access to receptive females. In Scotland's Moray Firth, bottlenose dolphins have been observed pursuing, butting and flicking harbour porpoises into the air. This could be a form of play, or a way to protect their territory and food resources from other cetaceans. Adult females may gang together to fend off a single medium-sized shark by head butting it. Shark attacks are a common cause of death among dolphin calves.

HUNTING STRATEGY

Along with humpback and killer whales, bottlenose dolphins exhibit some of the most sophisticated hunting behaviour of any cetacean. In South Carolina, for example, some inshore groups regularly encircle schools of fish and drive them toward the shallows in rivers and estuaries. Eventually the frightened fish run aground and the dolphins follow them, temporarily beaching themselves to pick the fish off the shore, and then wriggle to get themselves back into the water. Elsewhere, common bottlenoses herd fish into tighter and tighter schools, and then plunge through the panicking school to pick off the fish.

Coastal common bottlenose dolphins tend to feed on fish and invertebrates, such as crabs and octopuses, that live on or near the seabed. Offshore animals eat fish and squid from surface waters and mid-waters, at times diving to more than 500 m (1,600 ft) to do so. In some localities, dolphins have learned to follow fishing vessels and take advantage of the damaged or discarded catch, or those fish that have avoided the net but are temporarily disoriented or exhausted. Off Santa Catarina Island, Brazil, bottlenose dolphins even help herd fish toward the waiting nets of fishermen and are rewarded by being given part of the catch.

Above: Common bottlenose dolphins in South Carolina catching fish by scattering and stranding them.

INTELLIGENCE

Size for size, the brain of a bottlenose dolphin is about half the size of a human's. A high proportion of the dolphin brain's processing power is dedicated to interpreting sounds and the returning echoes of its echolocation mechanism. A variety of evidence suggests that bottlenose dolphins are intelligent – that is, their behaviour is highly adaptable and they can improvise according to circumstances. In oceanariums, dolphins are trained to perform complex tricks (although others would argue that their willingness to do so is an argument against their being intelligent). In experiments conducted in Hawaii with captive bottlenose dolphins, individuals are able to construct precise word commands by pressing levers in specific sequences, which shows understanding of meaning and expression of intent. Wild Indo-Pacific dolphins in Shark Bay, Western Australia, have been observed using a tool – a sponge that is held in the beak to protect the animal when searching for spiny prey on a rough, sandy seabed. Individuals in the group learn this behaviour from others.

Striped Dolphin

This beautifully marked dolphin is the species most often depicted in the frescoes of ancient Greece. It remains a common offshore species in the waters of the Mediterranean Sea and in warm temperate and tropical waters elsewhere. In real life, the delicate markings on the dolphin's side look almost hand-painted. Its most distinctive feature is a thin, dark stripe extending from the dark beak, around the eye and then along the lower flank, where it finally widens. A shorter stripe extends from the eye to the flipper. Both these major stripes may have a smaller stripe associated with them. The common dolphin is of a similar size and shape to the striped dolphin, but the common dolphin has a distinctive yellow hourglass pattern on its sides.

Like other dolphins of the genus *Stenella*, striped dolphins are acrobatic leapers, sometimes somersaulting or tailspinning. They occasionally swim above schools of yellowfin tuna or prey animals such as anchovies, causing them to be caught by fishermen as bycatch. Some inshore populations are threatened by pollution and by overfishing, which has reduced their supply of food.

Above: Striped dolphin leaping in the Gulf of Mexico, North Atlantic Ocean.

WHERE TO WATCH

Watching choice: Ligurian Sea, in the Mediterranean Sea between France and Italy.

When to go: April to September.

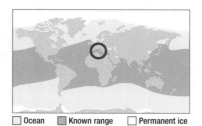

☐ Ocean　■ Known range　☐ Permanent ice

Getting there: Part-day excursions to multi-day research volunteer trips leave from local Italian ports such as San Remo, Andora and Finale Ligure. The nearest airports are Nice, France, and Genoa, Italy.

FACTFILE

Scientific name: *Stenella coeruleoalba*
Family: Delphinidae
Range: Warm temperate to tropical waters of the Atlantic, Indian and Pacific oceans
Habitat: Offshore or deep water close to land
Status: Common
Population: In excess of 750,000
Diet: Squid, fish and crustaceans
Length: 1.8–2.6 m (6–8½ ft)
Weight: 90–150 kg (200–330 lbs)

IDENTIFICATION

 Flukes have concave trailing edges and a notch in the middle. Pale grey above and below.

 Dorsal fin is grey or brown and moderately tall with a concave trailing edge.

 Flippers are narrow, tapered and grey or brown in coloration.

 A dark prominent beak with a distinct crease above. The lower forehead is pale grey and the upper forehead is grey or brown.

 Upper body is grey or brown, with pale grey extending up from the middle flank toward the dorsal fin and also across the rear body. A thin, dark stripe extends from the beak, around the eye, and along the lower flank, where it widens. A shorter stripe extends from the eye to the flipper. Underside is white or pink.

 Usually travel in groups of 25–100, and occasionally in groups of several hundred.

 May bow-ride. Acrobatic and may somersault or tail-spin when leaping and even porpoise upside-down. Occasionally dives to depths of 200 m (660 ft) for 5–10 minutes in search of mid-water fish and squid.

IDENTIFICATION

 Flukes have concave trailing edges and a notch in the middle. Black or grey above and below.

 Dorsal fin is moderately tall with a concave trailing edge. Can be black, grey or even centrally pale.

 Flippers are black or grey with a convex leading edge.

 In the short-beaked form, the forehead is quite domed and the beak is of moderate length and boldly marked. In the long-beaked form, the forehead is less domed and the beak slightly longer and less boldly marked.

 The dark grey or brown upper body pattern forms a V-shape below the dorsal fin. A yellowish patch on the mid-flank of the front half of the body and a similar-sized grey patch on the rear half produce a distinctive 'hourglass' shape. The lower flanks grade to pale on the underside of the front two-thirds of the body.

 Usually travel in groups of 10–200, and occasionally up to several thousand. Schools of long-beaked species tend to be smaller than those of short-beaked.

 Both species are acrobatic and may bow-ride, breach or porpoise. Their high-pitched squeals and whistles can occasionally be heard above the water surface.

Common Dolphin

Above: Long-beaked common dolphins porpoising in False Bay, South Africa.

This handsome dolphin, as its name suggests, is common in many parts of the world. It is of similar size and shape to several other prominently beaked dolphins. Its yellowish patch on the flank in the front half of the body and its similar-sized grey patch in the rear half give it a distinct 'hourglass' pattern that sets it apart from other species. The common dolphin is, in fact, at least two species: a short-beaked form (*Delphinus delphis*), which is widely distributed in warmer waters and occurs both offshore and inshore, and a long-beaked form (*Delphinus capensis*), which has a more limited distribution and prefers coastal waters.

The two species can be difficult to tell apart in the wild. The short-beaked form (see illustration below) has a slightly stubbier and more boldly marked beak, brighter body coloration, a slightly more domed forehead and a slightly stockier body than the long-beaked form. There are subtle behavioural differences between the two species.

FACTFILE

Scientific name: *Delphinus delphis* (short-beaked); *Delphinus capensis* (long-beaked)
Family: Delphinidae
Range: Warm temperate to tropical waters in Atlantic, Indian and Pacific oceans
Habitat: Coastal and oceanic
Status: Both species locally common
Population: Unknown
Diet: Mostly schooling fish and squid
Length: 1.8–2.6 m (6–8½ ft)
Weight: 90–150 kg (200–330 lbs)

WHERE TO WATCH

Watching choice: Gulf of California and lagoons of Baja California, Mexico, to see both species.
When to go: March to September.
Getting there: Boat- and/or shore-based whale-watching tours operate out of San Diego, La Paz, Ensenada, Rosarito and Tijuana. Major regional transport hubs are San Diego, Tijuana and La Paz.

☐ Ocean   ▨ Short-beaked common dolphin
☐ Permanent ice   ▨ Long-beaked common dolphin
▨ Overlap area

Spotted Dolphin

FACTFILE

Scientific name: *Stenella attenuata* (pantropical);
Stenella frontalis (Atlantic)
Family: Delphinidae
Range: Tropical to warm temperate Atlantic Ocean; similar
waters in Indian and Pacific oceans (pantropical only)
Habitat: Coastal to oceanic
Status: Both species locally common
Population: Unknown
Diet: Mostly schooling fish and squid
Length: 1.8–2.6 m (6–8½ ft); Atlantic smaller
Weight: 90–115 kg (200–255 lbs); Atlantic heavier

IDENTIFICATION

 Flukes have swept-back leading edges and fairly
straight trailing edges curved at the ends. There is a
notch in the middle. Grey above and below.

 Dorsal fin is grey. Straight or convex on leading edge
and strongly concave on trailing edge.

 Grey flippers. Curved leading edges and pointed tips.

 Beak is grey on upper side, paler on lower. Dark stripe
extends from beak to the eye, and is usually darker
and extends to the flipper in pantropical form. Upper
forehead is dark grey, lower forehead lighter grey.

 Dark grey cape from shoulders to beyond dorsal fin.
Lighter grey area across middle flank. Paler region
along lower flank and underside. Variable spotting is
more extensive in adults and darker on Atlantic species.

 Pantropical species travel in groups of 5–20 and often
assemble in larger groups of several hundred or even
thousands. Atlantic species gathers in smaller groups.

 Both species often bow-ride. Fast-swimming and very
acrobatic. Sometimes breach high in the air.

Left: A group of Atlantic spotted dolphins viewed underwater. Notice the
variation in colour and spotting between individuals.

There are two species of spotted dolphin. The
pantropical spotted dolphin (*Stenella attenuata*) is
widely distributed in tropical to warm temperate waters,
and the Atlantic spotted dolphin (*Stenella frontalis*),
shown in the illustration below, is found in similar waters,
but only in the Atlantic, where it is difficult to tell the
two species apart. Adult Atlantic spotted dolphins tend
to be stockier and spottier, with a dark cape that does
not extend as far down the flanks as it does in the
pantropical species. The pantropical form often has a
dark stripe extending from the lower beak to the flipper.

In both species, the spots develop as the animal
matures. Immature individuals can be mistaken for
bottlenose dolphins, but spotted dolphins tend to have
a darker cape. In both pantropical and Atlantic spotted
dolphins there is variation in colour, degree of spotting
and size, with coastal forms tending to be slightly larger
and to have thicker beaks than oceanic forms.

As with other *Stenella* dolphins, spotted dolphins
take frequent opportunities to bow-ride, breach or
otherwise play at the sea surface. Like other *Stenella*
species, dolphin schools often swim with tuna and are
sometimes caught as bycatch by fishermen.

WHERE TO WATCH

Watching choice:
Grand Bahama
Island, Bahamas,
North Atlantic Ocean.
When to go: May
to September.
Getting there:
Several-day tours leaving
from Dania, Fort
Lauderdale and other locations in Florida, or operating from
Freeport, Port Lucaya or West End on Grand Bahama Island.

☐ Ocean
☐ Permanent ice
▨ Pantropical spotted dolphin
▨ Atlantic spotted dolphin
▨ Overlap area

Northern and Southern Rightwhale Dolphins

FACTFILE

Scientific name: *Lissodelphis borealis* (northern); *Lissodelphis peronii* (southern)
Family: Delphinidae
Range: Northern Pacific (northern); cooler waters of southern Atlantic, Indian and Pacific oceans (southern)
Habitat: Offshore and oceanic
Status: Both species locally common
Population: Unknown for both species
Diet: Mostly near-surface and mid-water fish and squid
Length: 2.3–3 m (7½–10 ft); males larger than females
Weight: 80–120 kg (180–260 lbs)

IDENTIFICATION

 Flukes have concave trailing edges and a notch. Dark edges with white above and below (southern); white edges with dark above and white below (northern).

 No hint of a dorsal fin in either species.

 Flippers are tapered and white, with dark coloration above in the northern species.

 Short, well-defined beak. In northern species, the head is mostly black except for a pale patch on the underside of the beak. In southern species, the head is white up to the eye level and the middle of the forehead.

 Black body with a white underside. In southern species, the white coloration extends to about halfway up the flanks in the rear half of the body.

 Usually travel in groups of 100–200, but up to 3,000.

 Both species occasionally bow-ride. May breach, belly-flop, side-slap or lobtail. Swim in tight formation when fleeing. Dives may last 6 minutes or more.

Left: Three southern rightwhale dolphins leaping in Chilean waters.

Rightwhale dolphins, with their bold black-and-white coloration, lack of a dorsal fin and sleek body, are highly distinctive. Observers sometimes describe them as 'eel-like', as they leap low over the waves and seem to bounce along on the sea surface. They are more likely to be confused with seals, sea lions or, in the southern species, penguins, than with other dolphins.

The southern species (see photo opposite) has white flippers, a pale head and beak, and a large white patch extending up each flank. In the northern species (see illustration below), the white coloration is restricted mostly to the underside, and the flippers, head and beak are largely or entirely black.

Rightwhale dolphins hunt for bioluminescent (light-producing) fish and squid that are associated with the twilight zone at depths beyond 200 m (660 ft). Like some other oceanic cetaceans, rightwhale dolphins are sometimes caught in illegal drift nets. When caught this way, many members of the group are killed at the same time, and this may reduce the genetic variability of the species.

WHERE TO WATCH

Watching choice: Monterey Bay, California for the northern rightwhale dolphin.
When to go: April to October.
Getting there: Offshore whale-watching excursions leave from Monterey and Santa Cruz. The regional transport hub is San Francisco.

☐ Ocean ☐ Permanent ice ▨ Northern rightwhale dolphin ▨ Southern rightwhale dolphin

Long-Snouted Spinner Dolphin

The spinner dolphin, also known as the long-snouted spinner, is named for its aerial displays, when it rotates on its long axis as though, as one historical observer described it, 'spinning on a spit'. This behaviour, particularly evident when a group of dolphins scatters, is probably a communication to other individuals.

The spinner, with its sleek body, long beak, tall, curved dorsal fin and three-tone body pattern, is found inshore and far out to sea in warm waters. There are four subspecies of spinner dolphin – the eastern, Costa Rican, Hawaiian and dwarf spinner – and there is considerable variation in size and patterning among them. In the Atlantic Ocean, spinner dolphins can be mistaken for the clymene dolphin, also called the short-snouted spinner dolphin, because it occasionally spins. The clymene dolphin has a noticeably stubbier beak and a dark band across the upper flank that forms a V-shape beneath the dorsal fin, rather like that of a common dolphin.

Above: A spinner dolphin leaping in the waters near Hawaii.

WHERE TO WATCH

Watching choice: Hawaii (big island).
When to go: All year round.
Getting there: Kona Airport at Keahole on the big island (Hawaii) can be reached directly or by short flight from Honolulu Airport, on the nearby island of Oahu. Suitable boat excursions leave the big island from Honokohau, Kailua-Kona, Keauhou and Kohala Coast.

☐ Ocean ■ Known range ☐ Permanent ice

FACTFILE

Scientific name: *Stenella longirostris*
Family: Delphinidae
Range: Tropical and subtropical waters of the Atlantic, Indian and Pacific oceans
Habitat: Mainly offshore
Status: Locally common
Population: Well in excess of 1 million
Diet: Squid, fish and crustaceans
Length: 1.7–2.4 m (5½–8 ft)
Weight: 45–75 kg (100–165 lbs)

IDENTIFICATION

 Flukes have swept-back leading edges and fairly straight trailing edges curved at the ends. There is a notch in the middle. Grey above and below.

 Dorsal fin is dark grey and moderately tall. Shape ranges from nearly triangular to curved.

 Flippers are grey, narrow and tapered.

 Beak is grey, long and narrow, with a crease where it joins the forehead. Lower forehead is pale grey; upper forehead is darker grey. Chin is pale grey to white.

 Body has a three-tone pattern. Upper body is dark grey, sides a lighter grey and lower flanks and part of the belly are pale.

 Usually travel in groups of 5–200, and occasionally in groups of more than 1,000. Sometimes associate with yellowfin tuna and other species of dolphin.

 Often bow-ride for many minutes. Very acrobatic and often leap several times in a row. When a group scatters, individuals sometimes spin 2–4 times on their long axis as they leap through the air.

Tucuxi

FACTFILE

Scientific name: *Sotalia fluviatilis*
Family: Delphinidae
Range: Southern Brazil to Panama
Habitat: Coastal, river and lake waters
Status: Locally common
Population: Unknown
Diet: Small fish, squid and octopuses
Length: 1.4–2.1 m (4½–7 ft); freshwater subspecies smaller than coastal
Weight: 40–70 kg (90–155 lbs); freshwater subspecies lighter than coastal

IDENTIFICATION

 Flukes have concave trailing edges and a notch in the middle. Blue-grey above and below.

 Almost triangular dorsal fin in the middle of the back, sometimes curving slightly at the tip.

 Flippers are blue-grey or brownish grey, and are fairly broad.

 Beak is long, like that of a bottlenose dolphin, but with a straight mouthline. Upper beak is dark, underside is pale. Forehead is slightly rounded.

 Body is grey, with darker shades along the back gradually grading to paler grey on the lower flanks and underside.

 Usually in groups of 2–7, and occasionally up to 12 in freshwater or 30 along the coast.

 Does not bow-ride, but may wake-ride, leap, porpoise, spyhop, flipper-slap and lobtail. When diving rather than travelling, surfaces to breathe every 30–60 seconds.

Left: A tucuxi swimming in a small lake in Brazil. Notice its similarity to a bottlenose dolphin.

The tucuxi (pronounced 'too-koo-shi') is the smallest dolphin with a prominent beak. It looks like a dwarf version of a bottlenose dolphin, but with a relatively shorter and more triangular dorsal fin.

Found in eastern Central American and northeast South American coastal waters and some rivers and lakes, some tucuxis (classified as the subspecies *Sotalia fluviatilis fluviatilis*) live their entire lives in freshwater and are slightly smaller than the coastal subspecies (*Sotalia fluviatilis guianensis*). The freshwater tucuxi is easy to tell apart from the much larger boto, or Amazon river dolphin, with which it shares its habitat. Unlike the boto, the freshwater tucuxi stays in the main river channel when the river floods the surrounding forest. The coastal tucuxi is similar to a franciscana, a species of river dolphin that overlaps with the tucuxi's range, but the franciscana is bigger, with a much longer snout and squarish flippers.

The tucuxi, though locally abundant and widespread, is under threat in parts of its range. When rivers are dammed, the population of local dolphins is split into smaller separate populations, which are less likely to survive because of inbreeding. Along coasts, entanglement in fishing nets and pollution threaten their survival.

WHERE TO WATCH

Watching choice: Santa Catarina Island, Brazil.
When to go: June to October, when southern right whales are also viewable in the locality.

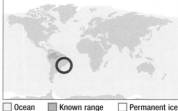

☐ Ocean   ■ Known range   ☐ Permanent ice

Getting there: Boat trips leave from ports on Santa Catarina Island. São Paulo and Rio de Janeiro are regional transport hubs.

Watching River Dolphins

Above: A close-up of the head of an Amazon river dolphin, or boto, showing the long narrow beak and bulbous forehead.

Below: A Ganges river dolphin showing the physical features characteristic of river dolphins in general.

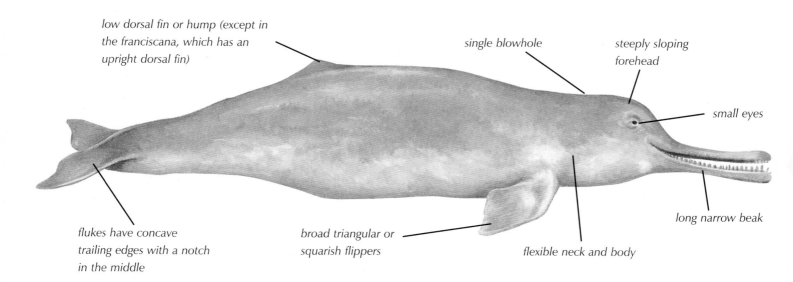

low dorsal fin or hump (except in the franciscana, which has an upright dorsal fin)

single blowhole

steeply sloping forehead

small eyes

long narrow beak

flukes have concave trailing edges with a notch in the middle

broad triangular or squarish flippers

flexible neck and body

The four species of river dolphin, with their bulbous foreheads and long beaks, resemble each other but are not closely related. Each species belongs to a separate cetacean family. Two species are South American; two are Asian. Their similarity originates, at least in part, from living in muddy freshwater or coastal waters and adapting to the conditions in similar ways. Three of the four species have poor eyesight, and all rely heavily on echolocation to navigate and find food. One of the four species, the franciscana, despite being called a river dolphin, does not enter rivers but stays in coastal waters.

RIVER DOLPHINS

BOTO (AMAZON RIVER DOLPHIN)
Grey or pink body. Low dorsal ridge, bulbous forehead and long, narrow beak. Amazon and Orinoco river systems.

BAIJI (YANGTZE RIVER DOLPHIN)
Blue-grey back and upper sides, pale underside. Sloping forehead and slightly upturned beak. Yangtze River, China.

GANGES AND INDUS RIVER DOLPHINS
Grey or brown body. Dorsal hump, sloping forehead and a beak that widens near tip with teeth exposed. Ganges (largely in India), Indus (Pakistan) and adjacent river systems.

FRANCISCANA (LA PLATA DOLPHIN)
Greyish brown. Small head, sloping forehead and long, straight beak. Upright dorsal fin. Coastal and estuarine waters between southern Brazil and northern Argentina.

IDENTIFICATION

The river dolphins are unlikely to be mistaken for other cetaceans in the few locations where they are found. They are quite small animals – typically less than 2.6 m (8½ ft) long. Compared to any oceanic dolphins with which they might be confused, they are slow moving and rarely engage in acrobatic surface behaviour. They can be recognised by their distinctive long, narrow beaks, which sometimes rise above the water surface. In a quiet river, dolphins can sometimes be heard. Their sneeze-like blows are typically repeated at 15- to 45-second intervals.

LOCAL KNOWLEDGE

Because of their limited distribution and shy habits, local knowledge is vital to increasing the chances of seeing one of these rare animals. In the Amazon, for example, the dolphins' preferred habitat lies where eddies form at the confluence of two rivers. Dolphins also gather where fish populations become concentrated during the dry season. In a few places the dolphins have a close association with people, and may visit at specific times of the day. Without local knowledge, days can be spent looking for the dolphins without success.

UNDER THREAT

River dolphins live in freshwater and coastal habitats that are vulnerable to alteration by human activities. The threats to these dolphins are wide-ranging, and include pollution, hunting, accidental entanglement in fishing nets, collisions with vessels and – something that does not so catastrophically affect saltwater cetaceans – the damming of rivers. The construction of dams to provide water for irrigation and to control floods is a priority in some developing countries. However, it puts remaining populations of at least one species of river dolphin at grave risk of extinction. The Yangtze river, Ganges river and Indus river dolphins are so scarce, vulnerable and relatively inaccessible that watching excursions are not currently encouraged. We include them in the following pages because their story deserves to be told. The Yangtze river dolphin is the most endangered cetacean of all.

Boto (Amazon River Dolphin)

FACTFILE

Scientific name: *Inia geoffrensis*
Family: Iniidae
Range: Amazon and Orinoco river systems of Brazil, Peru, Colombia and adjacent countries
Habitat: Rivers, lakes and flooded forest
Status: Vulnerable
Population: Not known
Diet: Small fish and bottom-living invertebrates
Length: 2–2.6 m (6½–8½ ft)
Weight: 110–180 kg (240–400 lbs)

IDENTIFICATION

 Flukes have slightly ragged trailing edges and a notch in the middle. Pink or bluish grey above and below.

 Pink or bluish grey dorsal hump, rather than a dorsal fin.

 Flippers are pink or grey, broad and triangular.

 Head is pink or grey. The beak is long and may have short bristles on the upper and lower sides. Forehead is distinctly bulged. Eyes are small.

 Body is pink or grey and quite lumpy in appearance. Neck and body are flexible.

 The loud blow, like a sneeze or snort, may sometimes be heard.

 Solitary or in groups of 2–4, except when more gather to feed on concentrations of prey.

 Usually slow swimming. Surface activity is more likely in the early morning and late afternoon. Dive sequence may occur with only the melon and blowhole briefly visible or a much more obvious arch and roll, with the beak and melon appearing, followed by an arched back showing the dorsal hump.

The boto (the dolphin's Brazilian name) is one of the strangest-looking cetaceans. Its body is long and flexible, enabling it to manoeuvre around submerged trees when the river floods the surrounding rainforest. Its bulbous forehead can change shape with the animal's mood and its skin can flush pink when the animal is threatened or otherwise disturbed.

Botos are usually solitary or swim in groups of two to four, although more may assemble where fish are concentrated in small areas during the dry season. Sometimes botos are bold and curious and will approach people who are swimming or boating. At other times they are secretive and are barely visible when they surface to breathe.

The boto is the most abundant and widespread of the river dolphins. It exists as three subspecies: one in the Orinoco River system and two in the Amazon. Until recently, the traditional beliefs of the local people – who regard the dolphin with a combination of dread and respect, in part because of its devious-looking smile – protected the boto from being hunted. However, these views are changing, and dolphins are increasingly likely to be killed by fishermen who see them as competitors. Dam projects also threaten dolphin populations in some tributaries of the Amazon and Orinoco.

WHERE TO WATCH

Watching choice: Manaus, Brazil.
When to go: August to November (dry season).
Getting there: Flights to Manaus, and then several-day boat trips along the Amazon and its tributaries.

☐ Ocean ■ Known range ☐ Permanent ice

Left: A male and female boto seen from above, showing their characteristic long beaks, dorsal humps and broad, triangular flippers.

Baiji (Yangtze River Dolphin)

The Yangtze river dolphin, or baiji (pronounced 'bye-gee'), the dolphin's Chinese name, is probably the rarest and most endangered cetacean. Western scientists only became aware of its existence in the early 1900s, and since then its population has plummeted from more than 1,000 to possibly less than 100. Baiji are accidentally caught in fishing nets or impaled on hooks, or electrocuted when fishermen use electricity to catch fish. In the past they have been hunted for meat and for body parts used in traditional medicines. The construction of dams has split up the few remaining groups and prevented them from migrating to find fresh supplies of fish when fishermen overharvest local fish stocks. Underwater blasting, to widen and deepen channels, and domestic, agricultural and industrial pollution all have taken their toll on its population.

The baiji could be mistaken for the finless porpoise, which also occurs within its limited range. The finless porpoise is widespread in the Yangtze River system. It is usually darker than the baiji and has a blunt head and a long, very low dorsal ridge that is indistinct.

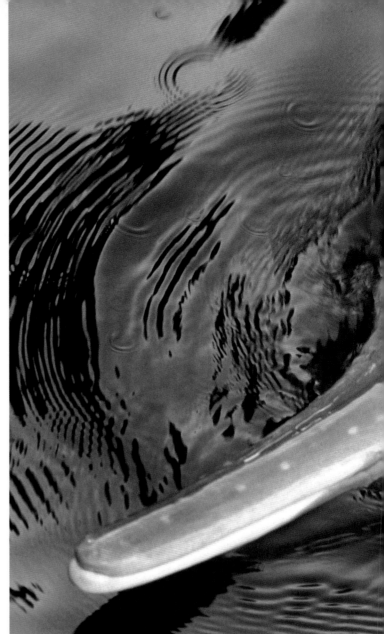

Above: The head and shoulders of a male Yangtze river dolphin that was kept in captivity from 1980 until its death in 2002.

CONSERVATION WATCH

Excursions to watch the baiji are not currently encouraged. Without human intervention, the baiji is likely to become extinct within 25–50 years. The Yangtze's

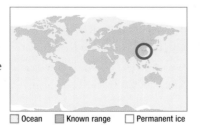

☐ Ocean   ▨ Known range   ☐ Permanent ice

Three Gorges dam, due for completion in 2008, will dramatically alter stretches of the river favoured by the baiji. Plans to transfer dolphins to enclosed waters where their well-being can be managed have so far met with little or no success.

FACTFILE

Scientific name: *Lipotes vexillifer*
Family: Lipotidae
Range: Lower 1,600 km (1,000 miles) of Yangtze River
Habitat: River, especially where tributaries enter
Status: Critically endangered
Population: Probably fewer than 100
Diet: Small fish
Length: 2–2.5 m (6½–8¼ ft)
Weight: 100–170 kg (220–370 lbs)

IDENTIFICATION

 Flukes are concave with a notch in the middle. Blue-grey above and pale below.

 Dorsal fin is bluish grey and roughly triangular with a blunt peak.

 Broad, triangular flippers. Bluish grey above and pale below.

 Head is blue-grey above and pale below. Beak is long and slightly upturned, giving the mouth the appearance of a smile. Forehead slopes strongly. Eyes are small.

 Body is blue-grey on the top half and grades to pale on the bottom half. The neck and body are flexible.

 The loud blow, like a high-pitched sneeze, can occasionally be heard.

 Solitary or, rarely, in groups of 2–4.

 Shy and easily frightened. Usually slow swimming. Surface activity is more likely between evening and early morning. When active, frequently swims on its back or side. Typical dive sequence is a long dive followed by several short breaths.

IDENTIFICATION

 Flukes are concave with a notch in the middle. Grey or grey-brown above and below.

 Dorsal hump rather than a dorsal fin is present. Grey or grey-brown.

 Flippers are grey or grey-brown, broad and triangular, with scalloped trailing edges.

 Head is grey or grey-brown. Beak is long and widens toward the tip, where the teeth are visible even with the mouth closed. Forehead slopes strongly. Eyes are very small.

 Body is grey or grey-brown and stocky. Neck and body are flexible.

 Solitary or occasionally in loose groups of 10 or more.

 Active during much of the day and night. Commonly shows the beak above the water. May breach and lobtail if disturbed. Dives typically last 30–90 seconds, but can last 3–5 minutes.

Ganges and Indus River Dolphins

The Ganges river dolphin, or susu, and the Indus river dolphin, or bhulan, were until recently classified as separate species. They are now regarded as two subspecies of the same species, *Platanista gangetica*. Although geographically separated, individuals of the two populations look the same and are genetically very similar. Until recently, the populations of the two dolphins were more widespread and probably interbred.

The tiny eyes of these river dolphins are unique among cetaceans in lacking a lens, making them unable to focus and see detail. The dolphins rely on their sophisticated echolocation system to 'see' in the turbid waters where they live.

The population and distribution of both subspecies have shrunk in the last century as a result of dam building, pollution and water extraction from rivers. The dolphins become entangled in fishing nets and, in some places, they are hunted as a source of meat and oil.

Above: A Ganges river dolphin in a tributary of the Ganges River in Bihar, India.

FACTFILE

Scientific name: *Platanista gangetica*
Family: Platanistidae
Range: Indus River system, Pakistan (Indus); Ganges, Brahmaputra and adjacent river systems in India, Nepal, Bangladesh and Bhutan (Ganges)
Habitat: Silt-laden rivers
Status: Endangered
Population: Unknown for the two subspecies
Diet: Mostly fish and shrimp
Length: 1.8–2.5 m (6–8¼ ft); females larger than males
Weight: 70–90 kg (155–200 lbs)

CONSERVATION WATCH

Excursions to watch the Ganges and Indus river dolphins are not currently encouraged. Although there are probably a few thousand Ganges river dolphins, the Indus subspecies numbers only a few hundred. A wildlife reserve has been set up for the Ganges subspecies, but protection is difficult to enforce. Without substantial human intervention to halt their decline, the future for both subspecies looks bleak.

☐ Ocean　■ Known range　☐ Permanent ice

Watching Porpoises

Although often overlooked by whale watchers because of their small size and relatively inconspicuous behaviour, porpoises can be just as engaging to watch as the larger and more expressive dolphins and whales. The name 'porpoise' – a contraction of the Latin *porcus* for 'pig' and *piscus* for 'fish' – refers correctly to a single family of small cetaceans, the Phocoenidae. The six species in this group lack beaks, have relatively small flippers and have spade-shaped rather than conical teeth. Porpoises live in coastal waters and rivers that bring them into frequent contact with people and their activities. Porpoises are losing out in competition with humans and many of their populations are declining.

IDENTIFICATION

Porpoises tend to be stouter than dolphins of similar size, have smaller heads and blunter jaws and lack a beak. Where a dorsal fin is present, it is more likely to be upright and without the concave trailing edge found in many dolphins. Porpoises lack the splashes of colour found in some dolphins, but the markings of some species are nevertheless striking. Except for the Dall's porpoise, porpoises rarely raise their bodies far out of the water.

Four of the six porpoise species tend to be quite shy and retiring, live in small groups, and usually avoid people. The Dall's porpoise in particular, and the finless porpoise to a lesser extent, may gather in large groups and may approach boats. Once a cetacean is suspected of being a porpoise, its identity is quite easy to pinpoint by a process of elimination. The six porpoise species live in different parts of the world, with only limited overlap in their geographic ranges.

UNDER THREAT

Most porpoises live in shallow coastal waters, estuaries and tidal rivers. These are habitats where the likelihood of encountering people and the effects of people's activities are high. As a result, porpoises tend to be subject to a wide variety of detrimental human-

Below: A harbour porpoise, showing the physical features characteristic of most porpoises.

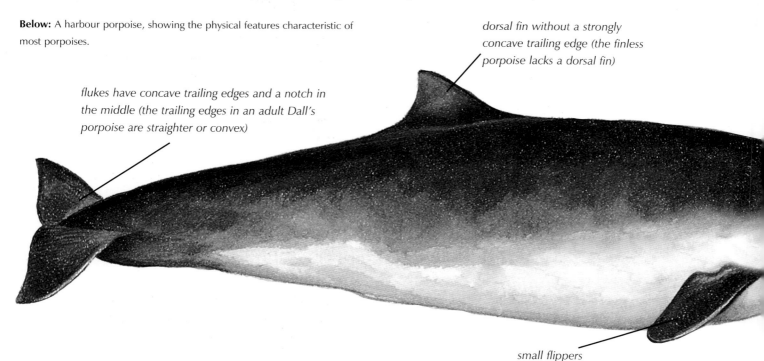

dorsal fin without a strongly concave trailing edge (the finless porpoise lacks a dorsal fin)

flukes have concave trailing edges and a notch in the middle (the trailing edges in an adult Dall's porpoise are straighter or convex)

small flippers

induced threats. These include pollution, boat traffic and habitat loss due to coastal building developments. The greatest threats probably come from entanglement in fishing nets and the removal of their food supply by overfishing. Various devices have been developed to scare porpoises away from entering nets, but these are not used in many areas where their deployment would be the most beneficial. Thousands of porpoises are still hunted in Japanese waters and elsewhere.

THE ENDANGERED VAQUITA

The dimunitive vaquita, *Phocoena sinus*, is like a smaller, paler version of the harbour porpoise. It is probably the world's smallest cetacean, reaching a maximum length of only 1.45 m (4¾ ft) and weighing 55 kg (120 lbs). It has the most restricted distribution of any marine cetacean, being found only at the northern end of the Gulf of California, Mexico. The common bottlenose dolphin and the long-beaked common dolphin frequent the same waters, but they have obvious beaks and are easy to distinguish from the vaquita.

The decline of the vaquita is linked to the fishing of a large species of sea bass, the totoaba, which is itself now endangered. In the 1920s an intensive fishery was developed to catch the totoaba. The large-mesh gill nets that were used also snared hundreds of vaquita. The commercial totoaba fishery was finally closed down in the 1970s. Since then, Mexico has established a biosphere reserve in the upper Gulf to protect the vaquita, the totoaba and other endangered species. However, the reserve is not adequately policed and both legal and illegal fishing for a variety of species still occur in the vicinity. This continues to take its toll on the vaquita and the fish on which it feeds. Probably 400 to 600 vaquitas remain, and they are critically endangered.

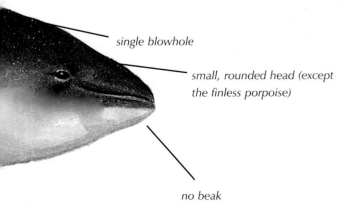

single blowhole

small, rounded head (except the finless porpoise)

no beak

PORPOISES

DALL'S PORPOISE
Large black-and-white porpoise. Dorsal fin is upright with a hooked tip. Northern North Pacific.

SPECTACLED PORPOISE
Black back and upper flanks. Brilliant white lower flanks and underside. Large, rounded dorsal fin. Cool waters in the Southern Hemisphere.

BURMEISTER'S PORPOISE
Black body with grey patches on underside. Dorsal fin is backward-sloping and set far back on the body. Temperate and subarctic coastal waters of South America.

HARBOUR PORPOISE
Black or dark grey back grading to pale underside. Dorsal fin has a slightly concave trailing edge. Temperate and subpolar waters of the Northern Hemisphere.

FINLESS PORPOISE
Dark grey or pale grey as adults. Bulbous forehead. The only porpoise lacking a dorsal fin. Coastal waters and major rivers of the Indo-Pacific.

VAQUITA
Grey back grading to pale underside. Dorsal fin has a slightly concave trailing edge. Found only at the northern end of the Gulf of California, Mexico.

Dall's Porpoise

FACTFILE

Scientific name: *Phocoenoides dalli*
Family: Phocoenidae
Range: Cool waters of the North Pacific
Habitat: Coastal and oceanic
Status: Locally common
Population: In excess of 200,000
Diet: Squid, crustaceans and schooling fish in mid-water
Length: 1.8–2.4 m (6–8 ft)
Weight: 135–200 kg (300–440 lbs)

IDENTIFICATION

 In adults, flukes have straight or even slightly convex trailing edges with a notch in the middle. Dark above and below, with trailing edges fringed with white or pale grey on the upper side.

 In adults, the dorsal fin is almost triangular, with a steep leading edge and a slightly hooked tip. Usually black at the base and pale grey near the tip.

 Flippers are small, black and close to the head. Sometimes the trailing edges are fringed with white.

 Head is black and beakless, with a sloping forehead.

 Stocky body. Mostly black except for a large white patch extending along the belly and flanks from just forward of the dorsal fin to the vent area. In some forms, the white extends as far forward as the flippers.

 Usually in groups of 2–10, but hundreds may gather at good feeding grounds. Sometimes swims with long-finned pilot whales or Pacific white-sided dolphins.

 May dart and zigzag at high speed and produce a 'rooster tail' spray when surfacing rather than cleanly porpoising. Inquisitive and may bow-ride or wake-ride.

Left: A Dall's porpoise viewed from above, producing the characteristic 'rooster tail' spray of water as it arcs through the surface.

The Dall's porpoise is much bulkier than other porpoises and, in its behaviour and choice of habitat, it is more like an oceanic dolphin than a coastal porpoise. Dall's porpoises can be inquisitive and will approach boats and bow-ride or wake-ride. They sometimes gather in large schools offshore. Almost hyperactive in their movements, they are probably the fastest-swimming small cetaceans, reaching speeds in excess of 48 km/h (30 mph).

With its stocky body and bold black-and-white coloration, Dall's porpoise is relatively easy to distinguish. The harbour porpoise is smaller, less social and does not have bold patterning. Like Pacific white-sided dolphins, Dall's porpoises produce a 'rooster tail' of spray as they arc through the surface. However, the dolphin has a strongly falcate (sickle-shaped and curved backward) dorsal fin and bold stripes on its flanks. At a casual glance, a Dall's porpoise could be mistaken for a killer whale, but orcas are much larger.

Dall's porpoise, although abundant and widely distributed, is often caught as a bycatch in fishing nets. Of more concern, since the moratorium on the commercial hunting of large whales, Japanese whalers have taken in excess of 10,000 Dall's porpoises a year.

WHERE TO WATCH

Watching choice: Vancouver Island, British Columbia.
When to go: May to September, when Pacific white-sided dolphins and killer whales are also viewable.
Getting there: Boat trips leave from Port Hardy, Port McNeill, Telegraph Cove and other ports on northern Vancouver Island. Vancouver is the regional transport hub.

☐ Ocean ■ Known range ☐ Permanent ice

Harbour Porpoise

The harbour porpoise is the only porpoise found in Europe. Although widespread in the Northern Hemisphere, it is regularly caught and drowned in fishing nets, so its distribution is now quite patchy. As coastal developments encroach on shallow waters, boat traffic increases and rivers discharge more pollution, the harbour porpoise's habitat is steadily diminishing and becoming degraded. Scientists chemically analyse the tissue of harbour porpoises to assess the degree of pollution in local waters.

An undemonstrative animal, the harbour porpoise is nevertheless a delight to those who have been able to observe it at close range. Sometimes slow moving, at others times fast swimming and agile, the harbour porpoise is usually glimpsed as it arcs smoothly at the water's surface. It is recognisable by its blunt head and medium-sized, almost triangular dorsal fin. The loud sneezing sound as it breathes has been likened to that of a puffing pig. It is one of the shortest-lived cetaceans, with few individuals surviving beyond 12 years.

Above: An underwater view of a harbour porpoise in the Irish Sea.

WHERE TO WATCH

Watching choice: West coast of Scotland and Western Isles.
When to go: April to October.
Getting there: Whale-watching tours, from half-days to a week or more, operate variously from Dervaig (Isle of Mull), Gairloch, Mallaig and Oban. Glasgow and then Oban are the main regional transport hubs.

□ Ocean ■ Known range □ Permanent ice

FACTFILE

Scientific name: *Phocoena phocoena*
Family: Phocoenidae
Range: Cool temperate to subarctic waters of the Northern Hemisphere
Habitat: Coastal waters, river estuaries and tidal rivers
Status: Locally common
Population: In excess of 400,000
Diet: Small schooling fish and squid
Length: 1.4–2 m (4½–6½ ft)
Weight: 55–75 kg (120–165 lbs)

IDENTIFICATION

 Flukes are concave with a notch in the middle. Grey above and below.

 Dorsal fin is grey. Triangular or with a slightly concave trailing edge.

 Flippers are small, dark and clearly visible against the pale body colour.

 Head is blunt and without a beak. Grey, with a pale chin. One or more dark lines run from the mouth to the flipper.

 Body is black or grey above, shading to pale below.

 The loud blow, like a high-pitched sneeze, can occasionally be heard.

 Usually in groups of 2–5.

 Usually shy and does not approach boats. Typical appearance is of a back rolling quickly through the surface, sometimes splashing, sometimes not. When travelling, typically breathes every 8–10 seconds. When feeding, dives of 2–6 minutes may be interspersed with 4–5 breaths at 10- to 20-second intervals. Occasionally leaps in an arc when chasing prey.

Finless Porpoise

FACTFILE

Scientific name: *Neophocaena phocaenoides*
Family: Phocoenidae
Range: Shallow waters of the Indian Ocean and western Pacific Ocean, from the Persian Gulf to Japan
Habitat: Coastal waters and some large rivers
Status: Locally common
Population: Not known
Diet: Fish, squid and shrimp
Length: 1.4–2 m (4½–6½ ft)
Weight: 35–70 kg (77–155 lbs)

IDENTIFICATION

 Flukes are concave with a notch in the middle. Grey above and below.

 Long, shallow grey dorsal ridge rather than a dorsal fin.

 Flippers are grey, broad and fairly pointed.

 Head is grey with a bulbous forehead. Mouth curves slightly upward. Many finless porpoises have pink eyes.

 Body is largely a single shade of grey, which may be dark in some populations or pale in others. Flexible neck.

 Solitary, in pairs or occasionally in small groups of up to 10. May gather in groups of up to 50 where the feeding is particularly good.

 Active, darting rapidly beneath the surface, but often shy and elusive. They usually reveal themselves by rolling at the surface to breathe, typically surfacing 3–4 times a minute when undisturbed. When feeding, or when disturbed, they may dive for 2–5 minutes.

This attractive porpoise – which looks rather like a small beluga – is shy and difficult to approach in much of its distribution in the shallow waters of the Indo-Pacific. However, in the Yangtze River system, they are accustomed to boat traffic and can be approachable.

The finless porpoise has at least two colour forms. Most animals, such as those in the South China Sea, are cream to light grey at birth and then darken to charcoal grey as they age (see illustration below). Finless porpoises in the Yangtze River are especially dark. In Japan and parts of northern China, calves are dark grey and then lighten as they mature, and may become almost as pale as a beluga (see photo opposite). The range of the finless porpoise overlaps with that of the Indo-Pacific humpbacked dolphin, which is a larger animal with a beak and an obvious dorsal hump.

Most finless porpoises live within 5 km (3 miles) of the coast. Residing close to large population centres, finless porpoises are subject to habitat degradation from boat traffic, dam-building, pollution and overfishing of their prey. The greatest cause of mortality is probably accidental entanglement in fishing nets. Despite being widespread, in many localities finless porpoise populations appear to be in steep decline, as in the Yangtze River system and the inland Sea of Japan.

WHERE TO WATCH

Watching choice: The North Lantau area of Hong Kong, China.
When to go: All year-round to see finless porpoises and Indo-Pacific humpbacked dolphins (locally called Chinese white dolphins).
Getting there: Porpoises and dolphins are viewable from the shore and on the more reputable dolphin-watching excursions. International flights to Hong Kong.

☐ Ocean   ■ Known range   ☐ Permanent ice

Left: A finless porpoise seen underwater. This individual is a pale adult. Notice its blunt head and its long dorsal ridge instead of a dorsal fin.

Glossary

Amphipod
A shrimp-like crustacean that belongs to the order Amphipoda. Amphipods living on or near the seabed are a food source for some cetaceans.

Baleen
Also called whalebone. It forms comb-like plates that hang down from the upper jaw of baleen whales. Fringes on the plates trap animal plankton and fish that the whale feeds upon.

Baleen whale
A member of the suborder of whales (Mysticeti) that have baleen instead of teeth.

Beak
The forward-projecting jaws of some toothed whales.

Blaze
A broad, light marking that usually runs diagonally below the dorsal fin.

Blow
Sometimes called a spout. A whale's out-breath, often visible as condensed water that forms a miniature cloud of spray above the whale's head.

Blowhole
An opening on top of the head where one or both nostrils exit.

Blubber
The layer of fat-rich tissue beneath a cetacean's skin. It acts as a heat insulator and energy store.

Bow-riding
The habit of some toothed whales or dolphins of riding the pressure wave in front of the bow of a vessel or the head of a large whale.

Breaching
The act of leaping out of the water and reentering with a splash.

Bycatch
Animals caught by fishermen that are not the intended catch.

Callosity
A raised area of rough skin on the head of a right whale. Barnacles and whale lice inhabit callosities.

Cape
A dark region on the shoulders and middle back of a cetacean that often extends partly down the flanks.

Cetacean
A marine mammal belonging to the order Cetacea. This includes all whales, dolphins and porpoises.

Community
The populations of organisms that live in a particular habitat.

Continental shelf
The submerged edge of a continent. It typically reaches an average depth of about 200 m (650 ft).

Copepod
A shrimp-like crustacean that is a member of the subclass Copepoda. A common part of the animal plankton, copepods are typically less than 12 mm (half an inch) long. They are among the most abundant animals in the sea and are food for some baleen whale species.

Crustacean
A member of the superclass of invertebrates Crustacea, which includes crabs, lobsters, barnacles, copepods and krill.

Current
A mass flow of water. Oceanic currents are generated by winds and the circulation of water produced by water-density differences.

Dolphin
A small cetacean with conical teeth. Dolphins belong to five families: Delphinidae, Platanistidae, Iniidae, Lipotidae and Pontoporiidae.

Dorsal fin
The fin on the back of a cetacean.

Dorsal ridge
A hump or ridge, rather than a distinct fin, on the back of a cetacean.

Drift net
An unanchored net, up to many miles long, that drifts in the water like a curtain to ensnare animals. Drift nets are unselective and capture many medium to large animals.

Echolocation
The mechanism by which toothed whales navigate and find food by emitting sounds and interpreting the qualities of the returning echoes.

Endangered
A species or population that is liable to become extinct within the foreseeable future, usually a matter of decades, unless people take preventive action.

Estuary
The body of water and its surroundings where a river meets the sea. In an estuary freshwater mixes with seawater.

Extinction
The dying out of all individuals in a population or species.

Falcate
The sickle shape of some dorsal fins. In such fins the leading edge is convex and the trailing edge concave.

Family
A scientific (taxonomic) grouping that contains one or more genera.

Flipper
Also called a pectoral fin. The paddle-shaped front limb of a marine mammal.

Flipper-slap
The act of raising a flipper out of the water and slapping it on the surface.

Flukes
The two horizontally flattened parts that make up the tail of a cetacean.

Fluking
The act of raising the flukes into the air just before diving.

Genus (plural: **genera**)
A scientific (taxonomic) grouping that contains one or more species.

Gill net
Similar to a drift net, but smaller and anchored in one place. Fish and other organisms swim into the net and become entangled in it.

Gulp-feeding
The method used by rorqual whales of engulfing a large volume of prey-laden seawater in one mouthful.

Habitat
The place where a species or community of organisms lives, and the environmental conditions associated with it.

Hybrid
An individual produced by interbreeding between two genetically different stocks, in the case of cetaceans, usually two different species.

Hydrophone
An underwater microphone.

Ice floe
A large, flat mass of floating, drifting sea ice.

Invertebrate
An animal without a backbone.

Krill
Shrimp-like crustaceans, called euphausiids, that make up part of the animal plankton, especially in cooler waters. Krill are typically 12 mm (half an inch) to 50 mm (2 in) long and make up the bulk of the diet of some baleen whales.

Latitude
Angular distance north or south of the Equator. High latitudes are poleward of 60°N or 60°S. Low latitudes are between the Equator and 30°N or 30°S. Mid latitudes are approximately between 30°N and 60°N, and 30°S and 60°S.

Lobtail
The act of a cetacean slapping the water surface with its flukes.

Logging
The act of a cetacean lying still at or just beneath the sea surface. A logging animal may be sleeping.

Mammal
A member of the vertebrate class Mammalia. Mammals are warm-blooded and have hair, and mothers suckle their young with milk.

Melon
The bulging forehead of a toothed whale. It also refers to the fat-rich organ beneath the forehead that is thought to be used for focusing sounds in echolocation.

Migration
The large-scale movement of animals from one place to another, often between breeding and feeding areas.

Mollusc
An invertebrate belonging to the phylum (major animal group) Mollusca. Includes bivalves such as clams and mussels, and cephalopods such as squid and octopuses.

Oceanic
Referring to the open sea beyond the continental shelf. The water depth here is usually greater than 200 m (650 ft).

Offshore
Well away from the coast.

Order
A scientific (taxonomic) grouping that contains one or more families.

Parasite
An animal that lives in or on another animal (its host) and gains food or other benefit at the host's expense.

Permanent ice
Expanses of ice around the North and South poles that do not melt away between one year and the next.

Phytoplankton
Plant plankton. Made up of drifting plants and plant-like forms, many of which are microscopic. Many phytoplankton are food for animal plankton (zooplankton).

Plankton
Organisms that drift in the water column. If they swim, they do so only weakly and cannot make progress against water currents.

Pod
A social group of cetaceans that moves in a coordinated fashion. It may refer to an extended family or friendship group, or a much larger group.

Polar
Referring to the area around the North or South poles. Polar waters are cold and usually contain ice for at least part of the year.

Population
Animals of the same species in a particular locality that interbreed.

Porpoise
A small cetacean belonging to the family Phocoenidae that lack a beak and have spade-shaped teeth.

Porpoising
Refers to the way smaller cetaceans leap out of the water in low arcs as they swim from one place to another.

Rooster tail
The conical spray of water that comes from the head of some dolphins and porpoises as they break the surface. It is especially characteristic of Dall's porpoises and white-beaked and Pacific white-sided dolphins.

Rorqual whale
A member of the baleen whale family Balaenopteridae. Rorqual whales have prominent throat grooves.

School
A group of aquatic animals that swims in a coordinated fashion. Often used in relation to fish, but may be applied to cetaceans.

Skim-feeding
A method of feeding used by right, bowhead and sometimes sei whales. It involves swimming along at, or just beneath, the sea surface, with the mouth open and continuously filtering seawater across the baleen.

Species
A group of individuals that look similar and interbreed naturally to produce fertile offspring. Populations of one species are more or less reproductively isolated from those of other species.

Spermaceti
The wax or oil obtained from the melon of a sperm whale. Previously used as a wax for candles or as an industrial lubricating oil.

Splashguard
A raised region just in front of the blowholes of a baleen whale. It helps prevent water splashing into the nostrils when the whale is breathing.

Spyhop
The act of a cetacean slowly raising its head vertically out of the water, probably to look around.

Stranding
A cetacean, either alive or dead, beaching itself on the shore.

Subarctic
Refers to a high-latitude transitional zone in the Northern Hemisphere between the Arctic and cool temperate regions.

Subpolar
Refers to the high-latitude transitional zones between polar and cool temperate regions.

Subspecies
A population of a species that is recognisably distinct, physically and genetically, from other populations of the same species.

Subtropical
Refers to mid-latitude region, between tropical and warm temperate. Typically, subtropical waters have an average annual temperature in the range 13–20°C (55–68°F).

Tail stock
The base of the tail in a cetacean. Strictly, it is the region behind the dorsal fin and forward of the flukes.

Temperate
Refers to mid-latitude regions between subpolar and subtropical. Typically, temperate waters have an average annual temperature in the range 10–13°C (50–55°F).

Toothed whale
A member of the suborder of whales (Odontoceti) that have teeth rather than baleen.

Tropical
Low-latitude regions between the tropics of Cancer (23°27'N) and Capricorn (23°27'S). Typically, tropical waters have an average annual temperature greater than 25°C (77°F).

Tubercles
Small bumps on the head and flippers of the humpback whale. Also found on the dorsal fin and flippers of some other cetacean species.

Vertebrate
An animal with a backbone.

Wake-riding
Swimming in the turbulence behind a moving vessel.

Water column
The water anywhere between the sea surface and the seabed.

Weaning
The process of a cetacean calf gradually giving up its dependence on its mother's milk.

Whale
Strictly, any member of the mammalian order Cetacea. In practice, only cetacean species that reach weights of greater than about a tonne are called whales. Smaller cetaceans are called dolphins or porpoises.

Whale lice
Also called cyamid crustaceans. They are members of the amphipod crustacean family Cyamidae and are parasites of some whales. They feed on whale skin.

Zooplankton
Drifting animal plankton, some of which are microscopic. Some zooplankton, such as copepods, are food for baleen whales.

Further Reading

BOOKS

Bright, Michael. *Dolphins*. London: BBC Worldwide, 2001.

Cahill, Tim. *Dolphins*. Washington, D.C.: National Geographic, 2000.

Carwardine, Mark. *Whales, Dolphins and Porpoises*. Rev. ed. London: Dorling Kindersley, 2000.

Carwardine, Mark. *Killer Whales*. London: BBC Worldwide, 2001.

Carwardine, Mark. *Guide to Whale Watching: Britain and Europe*. London: New Holland, 2003.

Cresswell, Graeme, and Dylan Walker. *Whales and Dolphins of the North American Pacific*. Hampshire: WILDGuides, 2004.

Cresswell, Graeme, Dylan Walker, and Todd Pusser. *Whales and Dolphins of the European Atlantic*. Hampshire: WILDGuides, 2006.

Day, Trevor. *Lakes and Rivers*. Biomes series. New York: Facts On File, 2006.

Day, Trevor. *Oceans*. Biomes series. New York: Facts On File, 2006.

Gill, Peter, and Cecilia Burke *Whale Watching in Australian and New Zealand Waters*. Rev. ed. Sydney, Australia: New Holland, 2004.

Hoyt, Erich. *Whale Watching 2001*. Yarmouth Port, MA: International Fund for Animal Welfare (IFAW), 2001.

Nybakken, James W. *Marine Biology: An Ecological Approach*. San Francisco: Benjamin Cummings, 2001.

Perrin, William F., Bernd Würsig, and J.G.M. Thewissen, Eds. *Encyclopedia of Marine Mammals*. San Diego: Academic Press, 2002.

Reeves, Randall R., Brent S. Stewart, Phillip J. Clapham, James A. Powell, and Pieter A. Folkens. *Sea Mammals of the World: A Complete Guide to Whales, Dolphins, Seals, Sea Lions and Sea Cows*. London: A & C Black, 2002.

Reeves, Randall R., Brian D. Smith, Enrique A. Crespo, and Giuseppe Notarbartolo di Sciara. *Dolphins, whales, and porpoises: 2002–2010 conservation action plan for the world's cetaceans*. Gland, Switzerland: The World Conservation Union (IUCN), 2003.

Simmonds, Mark. *Whales and Dolphins of the World*. London: New Holland, 2004.

Würtz, Maurizio and Nadia Repetto. *Dolphins and Whales*. Vercelli, Italy: White Star, 2005.

MAGAZINES AND SCIENTIFIC JOURNALS

Aquatic Mammals
The journal of the European Association for Aquatic Mammals.
www.eaam.org/aquamamm.htm

Discover
Science and technology magazine.
www.discover.com

Marine Mammal Science
New findings on marine mammals.
www.marinemammalogy.org/mms.htm

National Geographic
Articles on geography and conservation.
www.nationalgeographic.com

National Wildlife
Member magazine of the NWF.
www.nwf.org/nationalwildlife

Natural History
Articles on nature, science and culture.
www.naturalhistorymag.com

Nature
Features peer-reviewed research in all fields of science and technology.
www.nature.com/nature/index.html

New Scientist
A science and technology magazine.
www.newscientist.com/home.ns

Oceanus
Features articles on oceanography.
www.whoi.edu/oceanus/index.do

Science
Published by the American Association for the Advancement of Science.
www.sciencemag.org

Scientific American
Articles on science and technology.
www.sciam.com

Sea Frontiers
Published by the International Oceanographic Foundation.

Smithsonian
Features articles on nature and wildlife.
www.smithsonianmag.com

Useful Addresses

The following list is a general guide to whale-watching tours worldwide and is not a comprehensive listing. The publisher does not endorse any of the companies listed. Cetaceans are wild animals and some species are migratory, so sightings cannot be guaranteed. Sightings in certain areas may be seasonal and weather conditions are unpredictable. Check in advance when tours operate, and leave several days during which to take a whale-watching trip. See 'Responsible Watching' (pp. 22–3) for further information on selecting a trip. Addresses for tour operators and information centres listed are postal addresses: please contact directly for locations of tours.

ANTARCTIC

Peregrine Tours
First Floor, 8 Clerewater Place Lower Way
Thatcham
Berkshire RG19 3RF
United Kingdom
Tel: +44 (0)1635 872 300
Or
Peregrine Adventures
380 Lonsdale Street
Melbourne VIC 3000
Australia
www.peregrineadventures.com
Several marine mammal experts onboard. Tours last 10 nights and take in the South Shetland Islands and Antarctica.

ARCTIC

Aasiaat Tourist Service
PO Box 241
3950 Aasiaat
Greenland
Tel: +299 89 25 40
www.greenland-guide.dk/aasiaat-tourist
Whale-watching trips lasting two to six hours are available from July to September. The most frequently sighted whales are fin and humpback whales.

Nuuk Tourism
Hans Egedesvej 29
PO Box 199, 3900 Nuuk
Greenland
Tel: +299 32 27 00
www.greenland-guide.gl/nuuktour/default.htm
From June to October regular four-hour trips run to Nuuksfjord (Godthåbsfjord) to spot humpback whales.

Uummannaq Tourist Service
c/o Hotel Uummannaq
3961 Uummannaq
Greenland
Tel: +299 95 15 18
www.greenland-guide.dk/uummannaq-tourist/default.htm
Eight-hour trips to see fin, minke, killer and humpback whales from mid-July to November.

ASIA

Ogasawara Whale Watching Association (OWA)
Chichi-jima, Ogasawara-mura
Tokyo 100-2101
Japan
Tel: +81 (0)4998 23215
Tel: +81 (0)4988 22587 (for general information)
Helps manage and regulate whale watching on Ogasawara and also operates as an information centre.

Pamilacan Island Dolphin and Whale Watching Tours
Poblacion, Baclayon, Bohol 6301
Philippines
Tel: +63 (38) 5409279
www.dolphinwhalewatch.homestead.com
Tours aim to provide an alternative livelihood for families affected by the ban on hunting cetaceans.

Sea-Tac Whale and Dolphin Encounters
Ogasawara-mura
Japan
Tel: +81 (0)4998 2 2277
www.ogasawara.or.jp/sea-tac/eng/ourtour.html
Humpback-whale watching between January and April, and sperm-whale watching in September and October.

AUSTRALIA

Exmouth Visitor Centre
Murat Road
PO Box 149
Exmouth WA 6707
Tel: +61 (0)8 9949 1176
www.exmouthwa.com.au
Arranges bookings for humpback whale excursions
between July and November.

Imagine Cruises
123 Stockton Street
Nelson Bay NSW 2315
Tel: +61 (0)2 4984 9000
www.imaginecruises.com.au
Ecotourism certified tours from June to November.
Whales sighted include humpback, minke, southern
right, sei and Bryde's.

Moonshadow Cruises
Shop 3, 35 Stockton Street
Nelson Bay NSW 2315
Tel: +61 (0)2 4984 9388
www.moonshadow.com.au
Three-hour cruises from mid-May until late October.

The Oceania Project
PO Box 646
Byron Bay NSW 2481
Tel: +61 (0)2 6685 6128
www.oceania.org.au
Participate as a volunteer researcher on humpback
whale expeditions between August and October.

Sunrover Expeditions
Queens Beach, Scarborough QLD 4020
Tel: 1 800 353 717 (free call within Australia)
Tel: +61 (0)7 3880 0719
www.sunrover.com.au
Humpback whales sighted between May and October.

Sydney Eco Whale Watching
PO Box 6327
North Ryde NSW 2112
Tel: +61 (0)2 9878 0300
www.austspiritsailingco.com.au
Opportunities to see migrating humpback whales from
May to July and September to November.

Warrnambool Visitor Information Centre
Merri Street
Warrnambool VIC
Tel: 1 800 637 725 (free call within Australia)
Tel: +61 (0)3 5564 7837
www.warrnamboolinfo.com.au
Southern right whales can be viewed from land
between June and September.

Whalesong Cruises
PO Box 620
Hervey Bay QLD 4655
Tel: 1 800 689 610 (free call within Australia)
Tel: +61 (0)7 4125 6222
www.whalesong.com.au/cruises.htm
Half-day whale-watching tours from mid-July to
early November.

CANADA

Coastal Spirits Expeditions and Lodge Ltd
Box 630
Quathiaski Cove
Quadra Island, BC V0P 1N0
Tel: 1 888 427 5557 (free call within North America)
Tel: +1 (250) 285 2895
www.kayakbritishcolumbia.com
Operates the only base camp right beside a killer
whale reserve and rubbing beaches.

Ocean Explorations
Suite 316, 185–911 Yates Street
Victoria, BC V8V 4Y9
Tel: 1 888 442 6722 (free call within North America)
Tel: +1 (250) 383 6722
www.oceanexplorations.com
Half-day excursion from April to September
to see killer whales, as well as dolphins
and porpoises.

Prince of Whales Whale Watching
812 Wharf Street, Lower Causeway Level
Victoria, BC V8W 1T3
Tel: 1 888 383 4884 (free call within North America)
Tel: +1 (250) 383 4884
www.princeofwhales.com
Wildlife cruises leave regularly in search of killer, grey,
minke and humpback whales.

Seasmoke Whalewatching
PO Box 483
Alert Bay, BC V0N 1A0
Tel: 1 800 668 6722 (free call within North America)
Tel: +1 (250) 974 5225
www.seaorca.com
Choose between five- and eight-hour tours and four-hour motor cruises to view orcas in the core habitat waters of Johnstone Strait.

Surge Tours
Unit C, 157 Water Street
St Andrews, NB E5B 1A7
Tel: +1 (506) 529 4233
www.whale-watch-east.com
Working ecotours around the Bay of Fundy watching whales, seals and porpoises. Tours last between two and three hours.

Vancouver Whale Watch
Suite 210, 12240 Second Avenue
Steveston (Richmond), BC V7E 3L8
Tel: +1 (604) 274 9565
www.vancouverwhalewatch.com
Whale-watching tours with a professional naturalist. A portion of the proceeds supports local marine research.

EUROPE

Andenes Whale Centre
Hvalsafari AS
PO Box 58
Andenes 8483
Norway
Tel: +47 76 11 56 00
www.whalesafari.no
The Whale Centre includes a museum on whales and their biology, research and whaling. Whale safaris operate from May to September.

The Company of Whales
Longhill Maywick
Shetland ZE2 9JF
United Kingdom
Tel: +44 (0)19 5042 2483
www.companyofwhales.co.uk
Bay of Biscay tours from mid-June to September to see whales, dolphins, seabirds and sharks.

Dolphin and Whale Spotting
PO Box 92
230 Keflavik
Iceland
Tel: +354 421 7777
www.dolphin.is
Minke whales are commonly seen on three-hour trips.

Hebridean Whale and Dolphin Trust (HWDT)
28 Main Street
Tobermory
Isle of Mull PA75 6NU
Scotland, United Kingdom
Tel: +44 (0)168 8302 620
www.whaledolphintrust.co.uk
Lists whale-watching trips and land-based whale-watching sites in the Hebrides.

McKinlay Kidd
9 Dudley Avenue
Edinburgh EH6 4PL
Scotland, United Kingdom
www.seescotlanddifferently.co.uk
Tel: +44 (0)870 760 6027
Offers three-night tours. Marine biologists on board help you spot minke whales, dolphins and porpoises. You can assist by helping out with data collection.

Responsible Travel
Pavilion House
6 The Old Steine
Brighton
East Sussex BN1 1EJ
United Kingdom
www.responsibletravel.com
Ecotourism operator with whale-watching and conservation holidays available worldwide.

Whale Watch Azores
5 Old Parr Close
Banbury OX16 5HY
United Kingdom
Tel: +44 (0) 12 9526 7652
www.whalewatchazores.com
Sightings of sperm and short-finned pilot whales common. Blue, fin, sei, humpback, minke, northern bottlenose, pygmy sperm and false killer whales are also sighted.

The Whale Watching Patagonia Project
Pico Sport Lda, Frank Wirth
9950 Madalena
Pico Island, Azores
Portugal
www.patagoniaproject.net
Offers many wildlife tours that include whale watching.

MEXICO AND CARIBBEAN

Baja Adventure Company
603 Seagraze Drive
Oceanside, CA 92054
United States
Tel: 1 877 560 2252 (free call within U.S.)
Tel: +1 (760) 721 8433
www.bajaecotours.com
Whale-watching tours in Baja California, Mexico, between January and July.

Iguana Mama
Calle Principal 74
Cabarete, North Coast
Dominican Republic
Tel: 1 800 849 4720 (free call within US)
Tel: +1 (809) 571 0908
www.iguanamama.com
Adventure holidays that include whale watching.

The Whale Watching Center, Puerto Vallarta
Guerrero 339
Col. Centro, Puerto Vallarta
Jalisco, CP 48300
Mexico
Tel: 1 866 422 9972 (free call within North America)
Tel: +52 (322) 222 3310
www.vallartawhales.com
Humpback whale tours from December to March.

Wildlife Connection
Francia No. 140
Departamento 7 Col.
Versalles, Puerto Vallarta
Jalisco, CP 48310
Mexico
Tel: +52 (322) 22 536 21
www.wildlifeconnection.com
Observe whales and dolphins in Banderas Bay. Guides are professional biologists.

NEW ZEALAND AND SOUTH PACIFIC

Dolphin Watch Ecotours
Picton Foreshore
Picton
New Zealand
Tel: 0800 WILDLIFE (945 354 33) (free call within New Zealand)
Tel: +64 (0)3 573 8040
www.naturetours.co.nz
Offers a range of wildlife ecotours between October and April, with frequent sightings of bottlenose, dusky, Hector's and common dophins. Killer whales are also encountered.

Whale Watch
PO Box 89
Kaikoura
New Zealand
Tel: +64 3 319 6767
www.whalewatch.co.nz
Sperm whales are sighted year round. Migrating humpback, pilot, blue and southern right whales may also be seen.

Whaleswim Adventures
PO Box 551
Oneroa
Waiheke Island
Auckland
New Zealand
Tel/Fax: +64 (0)9 372 7073
www.whaleswim.com
Provides seven- and nine-day expeditions. Tours leave from Tonga between July and October to see humpback whales.

SOUTH AFRICA

Advantage Tours and Charters
PO Box 151
3936 KwaZulu-Natal
St Lucia
Tel: +27 (0)35 5901259
www.advantagetours.co.za
Three-hour tours operate from mid-May to late November. The majority of sightings are of humpback whales.

Hermanus Tourism Bureau
Tel: +27 (28) 3122629
www.hermanus.co.za
Provides information on watching southern right whales from May to December.

Ocean Safaris
PO Box 2194
Plettenberg Bay 6600
Tel: +27 (0) 44 533 4963
www.oceansafaris.co.za
Excursions to see dolphins and humpback, minke, Bryde's, southern right and killer whales. Tours operate year round, with whale sightings most common between July and November.

SOUTH AMERICA

Brazil Ecojourneys
Embratur SC.10.06.053.262/0001-09
Servidão Ilha Paraíso, 132
Campeche
Florianópolis SC
CEP 88063-555
Brazil
Tel: +55 (48) 32329270
www.brazilecojourneys.com
Whale-watching trips to see southern right whales between June and November.

Guacamayo Bahia Tours
Bolívar 902 y Arenas
Bahía de Caráquez
Ecuador
(Allow up to four weeks for mail to arrive.)
Tel: +593 52691107
www.riomuchacho.com
Trips to see humpback whales operate between July and September.

Patagonia-Argentina.com
La Tierra Como Solía Ser S.A.
956 Libertad St. Off. 22
Buenos Aires, C1012AAT
Argentina
Tel: +54 (11) 5236 4164
www.patagonia-argentina.com
Provides nformation on travel and whale-watching trips.

UNITED STATES

American Cetacean Society (ACS)
Whale Adventures
PO Box 1391
San Pedro, CA 90733-1391
Tel: +1 (310) 548 7821
www.acsonline.org
Offers several specialised whale-watching trips with certified naturalists throughout the year. Blue, humpback and killer whales are sighted.

Baja Expeditions, Inc.
2625 Garnet Avenue
San Diego, CA 92109
Tel: 1 800 843 6967 (free call within US)
www.bajaex.com
Trips to watch grey whales during their breeding, calving and nurturing cycle from early February to early April.

Boston Harbor Cruises
One Long Wharf
Boston, MA 02110
Tel: +1 (617) 227 4321
www.bostonharborcruises.com
Daily whale-watching tours from mid-April to the end of October. All trips are narrated by professional researchers from the Whale Center of New England.

Captain Bill's Whale Watch
24 Harbor Loop
Gloucester, MA 01930
Tel: 1 800 339 4253 (free call within US)
Tel: +1 (978) 283 6995
www.captainbillswhalewatch.com
Offers tours to see humpback whales from May to October. Trips include a pre-trip introduction to whale biology.

Island Adventures Inc.
Cap Sante Marina
Anacortes, WA 98221
Tel: 1 800 465 4604 (free call within US)
www.island-adventures.com
Provides trips to see killer whales. Routes are determined daily by the morning's whale information from the local sighting network.

Ocean Sports Waikoloa
PO Box 383699
69–275 Waikoloa Beach Drive
Waikoloa, HI 96738
Tel: 1 888 SAIL 234 (724 5234) (free call within US)
Tel: +1 (808) 886 6666
www.hawaiioceansports.com
Operates the Hawaiian Humpback Whale Center
all year round. Tours to see humpback whales
are seasonal.

Oceanic Society
Fort Mason Center
San Francisco, CA 94123
Tel: 1 800 326 7491 (free call within US)
www.oceanic-society.org
Tours to see grey whales off California from December
to May. Expert naturalists narrate.

ORGANISATIONS

American Cetacean Society (ACS)
PO Box 1391
San Pedro, CA 90733-1391
United States
Tel: +1 (310) 548 6279
www.acsonline.org
Protects cetaceans and their habitats through public
education, research grants and conservation actions.

America's Whale Alliance
PO Box 3040
Ashland, OR 97520
United States
Tel: +1 (541) 488 1883/482 1200
www.americaswhalealliance.org
American affiliate of the Global Whale Alliance, an
organisation dedicated to protecting the ban on
commercial whaling.

Convention on Migratory Species
United Nations Environment Programme (UNEP)
United Nations Premises
Martin-Luther-King-Str. 8
D-53175 Bonn
Germany
Tel: +49 (228) 815 2401/02
www.cms.int
Conserves migratory species throughout their range.

Eco Tourism Australia
GPO Box 268
Brisbane, QLD 4001
Australia
www.ecotourism.org.au
Eco Tourism Australia was formed in 1991 as an
incorporated nonprofit organisation, and is the
primary national body for the ecotourism industry.

Food and Agricultural Organisation of the
United Nations (FAO)
Viale delle Terme di Caracalla
00100 Rome
Italy
Tel: (+39) 06 57051
www.fao.org
Provides information on the impact of tourism,
hunting and other human activities on cetaceans.

Greenpeace International
Ottho Heldringstraat 5
Amsterdam 1066 AZ
The Netherlands
Tel: +31 20 7182000
www.greenpeace.org
A nonprofit organisation that campaigns against
enviromental degradation. See website for regional
office details.

GREMM
C.P. 223
108 de la Cale Sèche
Tadoussac, QC G0T 2A0
Canada
Tel: +1 (418) 235 4701
www.gremm.org
A nonprofit organisation dedicated to research
on the marine mammals of the St Lawrence
River area.

International Ecotourism Society
Suite 300
1333 H Street NW, East Tower
Washington, DC 20005
United States
Tel: +1 (202) 347 9203
www.ecotourism.org
Promotes responsible travel that conserves the
environment and improves the well-being of
local people.

International Fund for Animal Welfare
411 Main Street
PO Box 193
Yarmouth Port, MA 02675
United States
Tel: 1 800 932 4329 (free call within US)
Tel: +1 (508) 744 2000
www.ifaw.org
Promotes communication between communities, government leaders and like-minded organisations worldwide to advocate animal welfare and conservation.

International Whaling Commission (IWC)
Amsterdam 1066 AZ
The Netherlands
Tel: +31 20 7182000
www.iwcoffice.org
Provides for the proper conservation of whale stocks to make possible the orderly development of the whaling industry.

MarineBio.org
1810 Elmen Street
Houston, TX 77019
United States
www.marinebio.org
An evolving online tribute to all ocean life, marine biology and marine conservation.

Marine Conservation Society (MCS)
Unit 3, Wolf Business Park, Alton Road
Ross-on-Wye
Herefordshire HR9 5NB
United Kingdom
Tel: +44 (0)1989 566017
www.mcsuk.org
A UK-based charity dedicated to protecting the marine environment and its wildlife.

The Ocean Alliance and
The Whale Conservation Institute
191 Weston Road
Lincoln, MA 01773
United States
Tel: 1 800 96WHALE (969 4253) (free call within US)
Tel: +1 (781) 259 0423
www.oceanalliance.org
Dedicated to the conservation of whales and their ocean environment through research and education.

Ocean Conservancy
2029 K Street NW
Washington, DC 20006
United States
Tel: 1 800 519 1541 (free call within US)
Tel: +1 (202) 429 5609
www.oceanconservancy.org
Promotes healthy and diverse ocean ecosystems and opposes practices that threaten ocean life.

The Oceania Project
PO Box 646
Byron Bay, NSW 2481
Australia
Tel: +61 (0)2 66858128
www.oceania.org.au
A nonprofit research and education organisation dedicated to raising awareness about cetaceans and the ocean environment.

Organisation Cetacea (ORCA)
7 Ermin Close
Baydon, Marlborough, Wiltshire, SN8 2JQ
United Kingdom
www.orcaweb.org.uk
A registered charity that promotes conservation of the marine environment through research, partnership and education.

Orrca Inc.
GPO Box 362
Sydney, NSW 2001
Australia
Tel: +61 (0)2 9415 3333
www.orrca.org.au
Works with the National Parks and Wildlife Service to aid stranded whales. Volunteers operate the Orrca Hotline from home 24 hours every day for emergencies.

Sea Watch Foundation
11 Jersey Road
Oxford, OX4 4RT
United Kingdom
Tel: +44 (0)1865 717276
www.seawatchfoundation.org.uk
Aims to achieve better conservation for whales and dolphins in the seas around Britain and Ireland by promoting public awareness and involvement and by lobbying for better environmental protection.

SeaWeb
4th Floor, 1731 Connecticut Avenue NW
Washington, DC 20009
United States
Tel: +1 (202) 483 9570
www.seaweb.org
A nonprofit organisation that uses social marketing
techniques to advance ocean conservation.

TETHYS Research Institute
Istituto Tethys
c/o Acquario Civico
Viale G.B. Gadio 2
Milano 20121
Italy
Tel: +39 027 2001 947
www.tethys.org
A nonprofit NGO for study and conservation
of the marine environment.

United Nations Environment Programme (UNEP)
Regional Office for North America
Suite 300, 1707 H Street NW
Washington, DC 20006
United States
Tel: +1 (202) 785 0465
www.unep.org
Provides leadership and encourages partnership
in caring for the environment.

United Nations Environment Programme World
Conservation Monitoring Centre (UNEP-WCMC)
219 Huntingdon Road
Cambridge CB3 0DL
United Kingdom
Tel: +44 (0)1223 277314
www.unep-wcmc.org
Provides biodiversity information for policy and
action to conserve the living world.

Whale and Dolphin Conservation Society
Brookfield House
38 St Paul Street
Chippenham, Wiltshire SN15 1LJ
United Kingdom
Tel: 0870 870 0027 (free call within UK)
Tel: +44 (0)1249 449500
www.wdcs.org
A charity for the protection of cetaceans and
their environment.

Whale Watch Operators Association Northwest
PO Box 2404
Friday Harbor, WA 98250
United States
www.nwwhalewatchers.org
A group of companies dedicated to responsible
wildlife viewing.

The World Conservation Union (IUCN)
IUCN Headquarters
Rue Mauverney 28
Gland 1196
Switzerland
Tel: +41 (22) 999 0000
www.iucn.org
Encourages and assists societies throughout
the world to conserve the integrity and
diversity of nature and to ensure that any
use of natural resources is equitable and
ecologically sustainable.

World Resources Institute (WRI)
Suite 800, 10 G Street NE
Washington, DC 20002
United States
Tel: +1 (202) 729 7600
www.wri.org
Aims to move human society to live in ways that
protect the Earth's environment for current and
future generations.

World Wildlife Fund (WWF)
1250 Twenty-Fourth Street NW
PO Box 97180
Washington, DC 20090-7180
United States
Tel: +1 (202) 293 4800
www.worldwildlife.org
A nonprofit organaisation that leads international
efforts to protect endangered species and
their habitats.

Worldwide Fund for Nature
1196 Av. du Mont Blanc
Gland
Switzerland
Tel: +41 22 364 91 11
www.panda.org
The global arm of the World Wildlife Fund.
See website for country-specific contact details.

Index

Acknowledgements

PHOTOGRAPHIC CREDITS

NPL=Nature Picture Library Limited, OSF=Oxford Scientific Films, FLPA=Frank Lane Picture Agency
b=bottom, t=top, r=right

Front cover: NPL/Tom Walmsley;
Back cover: b Arctic Photos/Bryan and Cherry Alexander; t NPL/ Brandon Cole.

1 NPL/Doug Perrine; 3 Corbis/Paul A Souders; 6–7 John Hyde/Pacific Stock/OSF; 9t NPL Todd Pusser; 9b NPL/Jeff Foott; 11 NPL/Todd Pusser; 12–13 NPL/Doug Perrine; 14 NPL/Doug Allan; 17 NPL/Doug Perrine; 18t NPL/Gabriel Rojo; 18b NPL/Brandon Cole; 19t NPL/Brandon Cole; 19b NPL/Jeff Rotman; 20t NPL/Todd Pusser; 20b NPL/Brandon Cole; 20r NPL/Jurgen Freund; 21 NPL/Brandon Cole; 23 NPL/Jurgen Freund; 27 NPL/Georgette Douwma; 29 Getty/ Simon Parry/AFP; 30 Arctic Photos/Bryan and Cherry Alexander; 31 NPL/Brandon Cole; 32 Oxford Scientific Films/ John Hyde/Pacific Stock; 34 Tom Walmsley; 37 Corbis/Paul A Souders; 38–39 Flip Nicklin/Minden Pictures/FLPA; 40–41 NPL/Mark Carwardine; 43 Corbis/Paul A Souders; 44 Corbis/Ron Sanford; 45 NPL/Mark Carwardine; 46–47 NPL/Doug Perrine; 48–49 NPL/Doug Perrine; 50–51 FLPA/Rinie Van Muers/Foto Natura; 53 NPL/Armin Maywald; 54–55 FLPA/Flip Nicklin/Minden Pictures; 56 NPL/Gabriel Rojo; 58 NPL/Tom Walmsley; 60 NPL/Doug Perrine; 62–63 Amos Nachoum/Corbis; 64–65 Seapics; 66 NPL/Todd Pusser; 68–69 Graeme Cresswell; 70 FLPA/Flip Nicklin/Minden Pictures; 72–73 NPL/Todd Pusser; 74 and 76 Dylan Walker; 78–79 FLPA/Chris Newbert/Minden Pictures; 81–82 Flip Nicklin/ Minden Pictures; 84 Getty/Norbert Rosing/National Geographic; 86 NPL/Miles Barton; 88 NPL/Tom Walmsley; 90 NPL/ Sue Flood; 91 NPL/Brandon Cole; 92 NPL/Todd Pusser; 94 NPL/Doug Perrine; 96 NPL/Tom Walmsley; 98 NPL/ Mark Carwardine; 100–101 OSF/Keith Ringland; 102–103 NPL/Mark Carwardine; 104–105 Corbis/Stuart Westmorland; 106 NPL/Tom Walmsley; 108 NPL/Todd Pusser; 110 NPL/Tom Walmsley; 112 and 114 NPL/Doug Perrine; 115 NPL/ Neil Lucas; 116–117 NPL/Todd Pusser; 118–119 NPL/Mark Carwardine; 120 NPL/Doug Perrine; 122 Seapics; 124–125 NPL/Doug Perrine; 126 FLPA/Flip Nicklin/Minden Pictures; 128 NPL/Todd Pusser; 130 FLPA/Flip Nicklin/Minden Pictures; 132–133 NPL/Mark Carwardine; 134–135 NPL/Toby Sinclair; 138 NPL/Todd Pusser; 140 NPL/Florian Graner; 142 Seapics.

ARTWORK CREDITS

Artists:
Graham Allen
Fiammetta Dogi
Gill Tomblin
Dick Twinney